The Every Computer Performance Book

Bob Wescott

Dedication

This book is dedicated to my dear wife Sarah and all the other kind people who helped me on the way.

CONTENTS

Acknowledgments

No man is an island.

If there is anything amusing or useful to you in this book it flows from the great teachers I've had. Thank you Charles Butterfield and Bob Flegal. It flows from the truly gifted people I've worked with. Thank you Jacki Dibble, Allen Wright, Sharon Cunningham, Bill Peach, Otto Newman, Jan Parker, and Keith Smith. It flows from generous friends like Russell Aminzade and from the inspirational work of people I've never met. Thank you Alton Brown, Richard Feynman, Mr. Wizard, and Bill Nye - The Science Guy.

Preface

I'm not making this up.
I was in the big meeting before they let me on the live system that was at the very core of the second largest stock exchange in the United States. Everyone was there including the CIO. The meeting went smoothly and was very professional. When the meeting ended, the room cleared except for me and a powerfully built young man who was the lead system administrator. He got right in my face and in a clearly threatening tone quietly said, "Don't fuck up the computer!"

On another day, at another business, the CEO asked me into his office and quietly told me: "If you do not have this problem fixed by the end of the week, I will have to lay everyone off and sell the building." He was as serious as the grave.

On another day, on a different continent, I discovered the root of a huge problem a credit card company was having. A trivial change in the source code made a key transaction run approximately 200 times faster. The ensuing celebration was epic.

Performance work can make you a hero, it can save the company, and it can get you threatened, as well. However, most of the time it is remarkably ordinary. You gather data. You work to understand what it's telling you. You present your conclusions. If you do your work right, most of the time, there is no drama at all.

Any average person can do basic performance work. You can read the obvious meters and write nice little reports. If you have an inquisitive mind and the willingness to dig for the hidden truth, then you can go beyond the obvious meters and do great work – the kind of work that saves the company.

I have written this humble little book to give back the hints, tricks, knowledge, and wisdom so many have generously given to me. I believe it contains the fundamental keys to doing great performance work on any computer. I hope that you find them useful.

Chapter 1

WHY READ
THIS BOOK?

Life is short. Time is precious.

This chapter explains why you should read this book and how it can help you with any computer performance problem, now or in the future.

Good News!

Performance work is a great career because the only constant in this universe is change. Everything (hardware, operating systems, networking, applications, users, corporate goals, org charts, priorities, and budgets) changes over time and with change comes new performance challenges. There are always things to do, things to learn, things to prepare for, and experiments to run. Good performance work can save the company and put your kids though college. Yay!

Bad News...

Most computer performance books are fairly useless for solving your problems. Why? Because:

- Some have hundreds of pages of very difficult math that most people can't do and most problems don't require.

- Many focus on a specific version of some product, but you don't have that version.

- There is no performance book for a key part of your transaction path.

- There are so many different technologies in your transaction path; to read all the necessary books would take longer than the average corporate lifetime.

- Almost all manuals about a specific version of a technology were written under tremendous time pressure at about the same time the engineering was being completed; thus the engineers had little time to talk to the writers. The result is that these books document, but they don't illuminate. They explain the *what*, but not the *why*. They cover the surface, but don't show the deep connections.

So, How Is This Book Different?

Should you accept the bad news, stop reading here and switch careers? I don't think so.

There are some important differences in this book you should consider before deciding.

The Advice Is Timeless

What I'm about to tell you will work for any collection of computers, running any software that has ever been built. It will continue to be useful 100 years from now when today's technology, if it runs at all, will look as quaint as a mechanical cuckoo clock. How's that work?

Simple. The fundamental forces of the universe don't change over time.

Whether you are studying the slow response time of a computer, the root cause of a traffic jam, or why you are always in the slowest line, understanding those forces gives you a big insight into why this is happening. They help you make sense out of the performance meters you do understand and help keep you from making big mistakes.

It Works With Any Meters You Have

This book gives you tools to explore any available metering data. It shows you how to use the scientific method to

decipher what they mean and how to find patterns in the raw data. These patterns can tell you useful things about what's going on inside the giant black box that is your computing world. With this book you can turn raw data and weird meters into solid information that can solve and/or prevent serious problems.

It Helps You Find and Focus

Many parts of this book help you solve the diversity and

complexity problems mentioned earlier by helping you quickly determine that large chunks of your computing infrastructure are <u>not the problem</u>. This rapidly focuses your company's full and undivided attention on the small part of your computing world (System Z) that is causing the performance problem.

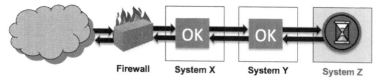

Once focused, a large fraction of everyone's effort is spent working in the right place and on the right problem. Now, the right experts can be consulted and business decisions can be made to fix or work around the problem.

The Math is Doable

All the math is boiled down to a few simple, wildly useful formulas. The most complex formula I use is:

$$R = S / (1 - U)$$

If you can replace **S** with the number **2** and **U** with the number **0.5** and calculate that **R** is equal to (spoiler alert) **4**, then you have all the math you need for a long career in performance.

It Helps With The Human Side Of Performance

In the future, money will still be important, humans will still want to avoid risk, office politics will still matter, and there will be many ways that you can be right, but still fail because you did not pay attention to the people involved.

Why Read This Book?

Having worked many performance problems from problem discovery, through solution presentation to senior management, and then on to problem resolution, I've made a few mistakes and learned a few tricks. They are all in here.

It Gets To The Point

This book is concise, useful, and occasionally funny. It gives you the tools needed to explore, and discover the hidden truths about your computing world. With it, and some work on your part, you'll be able to solve performance problems and to walk into the CIO's office with confidence.

Who Am I To Make These Claims?

If you are impressed with work experience, then read on as I've spent the last 25 years teaching performance fundamentals, capacity planning, modeling, and performance testing of websites. I spent about 15 of those years also doing performance work on live systems and critical applications for customers around the world. When working with customers I would typically spend 3-5 days there. I would arrive knowing almost nothing about their business and their problems and leave having given them a clear path to follow.

If you are a person who is only impressed with academic qualifications then I have few to offer you. I went to college with no particular plan, other than to have a good time. I had three majors (Wildlife Biology, Botany and Computer Science) but I have no degree as I left college when I ran out of money and got my first job in the computer industry.

I'm a practical guy that listens well, seeks out useful insights, tools and techniques. I've read a few computer performance books and found a few good things here and there. Mostly I've learned from other performance wizards, programmers, system administrators and a few generally smart people I've known. If it worked for them, then I'd figure out how to make it work for me.

I'm also good at explaining things clearly. I've had plenty of practice in my standup teaching as well as when working with customers. Clarity is essential when explaining to senior management that they need to spend large amounts of money. An engaging style is essential when teaching multi-day classes, especially just after lunch. I like people and if I couldn't make my classes useful, interesting, and relevant, then I would have stopped teaching a long time ago.

The seed idea of this book came from *Anybody's Bike Book* by Tom Cuthbertson. Back in the 70's he wrote this wonderful little book about repairing literally *any* bicycle. Forty years later, it is still in print and still useful.

Chapter 2

RIGHT TOOL
FOR THE JOB

There are the four fundamental tools used to explore and
solve performance problems.

This chapter discusses what they are, when to use them, and
how these tools interact.

The Four Tools of Performance

Your business depends on a collection of computers,
software, networking equipment, and specialized devices.
There are parts of it that you control and can directly meter.
There are many other parts that you don't control, can't
meter, and have no clue how they do their work.
Furthermore, there are limits placed on you due to politics,
time, budget, legal restrictions, and the tools you have
available.

All companies have an internal language and shorthand
terms they use when describing the subset of the entire
computing universe that determines their customer's

experience. Here we will just refer to that subset as the system. As a performance person you study this mysterious system and ask three questions: "What is the system doing now?", "Why is the system running slow?", and "Can the system handle the upcoming peak load?" To answer these questions you open your tool bag and discover four tools. Let me introduce you to them...

Performance Monitoring

Ignorance is not bliss.

Performance monitoring is about understanding what's happening right now. It usually includes dealing with immediate performance problems or collecting data that will be used by the other three tools to plan for future peak loads.

In performance monitoring you need to know three things: the incoming workload, the resource consumption and what is normal. Without these three things you can only solve the most obvious performance problems and have to rely on tools outside the scientific realm (such as a Ouija Board, or a Magic 8 Ball) to predict the future.

You need to know the incoming workload (what the users are asking your system to do) because all computers run just fine under no load. Performance problems crop up as the load goes up. These performance problems come in two basic flavors: *Expected* and *Unexpected*.

Expected problems are when the users are simply asking the application for more things per second than it can do. You see this during an expected peak in demand like the biggest shopping day of the year. Expected problems are no fun, but they can be foreseen and, depending on the situation, your response might be to endure them, because money is tight or because the fix might introduce too much risk.

Unexpected problems are when the incoming workload should be well within the capabilities of the application, but something is wrong and either the end-user performance is bad or some performance meter makes no sense. Unexpected problems cause much unpleasantness and demand rapid diagnosis and repair.

The key to all performance work is to know what is normal. Let me illustrate that with a trip to the grocery store.

The other day I was buying three potatoes and an onion for a soup I was making. The new kid behind the cash register looked at me and said: "That will be $22.50." What surprised me was the total lack of internal error checking at this outrageous price (in 2012) for three potatoes and an onion. This could be a simple case of them not caring about doing a good job, but my more charitable assessment is that he had no idea what "normal" was, so everything the register told him had to be taken at face value. Don't be like that kid.

On any given day you, as the performance person, should be able to have a fairly good idea of how much work the users are asking the system to do and what the major performance meters are showing. If you have a good sense of what is normal for your situation, then any abnormality will jump right out at you in the same way you notice subtle changes in a loved one that a stranger would miss. This can save your bacon because if you spot the unexpected utilization before the peak occurs, then you have time to find and fix the problem before the system comes under a peak load.

There are some challenges in getting this data. The biggest and most common challenge is in getting the workload data. The Performance Monitoring chapter will show you how to overcome challenges like:

- There is no workload data.

- The only workload data available (ex: per day **transaction** volume) is at too low a resolution to be any good for rapid performance changes.

- The workload is made of many different transaction types (buy, sell, etc.) It's not clear what to meter.

With rare exception I've found the lack of easily available workload information to be the single best predictor of how bad the situation is performance wise.

"The less a company knows about the work their system did in the last five minutes, the more deeply screwed up they are."
– Bob's First Rule of Performance Work

What meters should you collect? Meters fall into big categories. There are utilization meters that tell you how busy a resource is, there are count meters that count interesting events (some good, some bad), and there are duration meters that tell you how long something took. As the commemorative plate infomercial says: *"Collect them all!"* Please don't wait for perfection. Start somewhere, collect something and, as you explore and discover, add this to your collection.

When should you run the meters? Your meters should be running all the time (like bank security cameras) so that when weird things happen you have a multitude of clues to look at. You will want to search this data by time (What happened at 10:30?), so be sure to include timestamps.

The data you collect can also be used to predict the future with the other three tools in your bag: Capacity Planning, Load Testing, and Modeling.

Capacity Planning

Capacity planning is the simple science of scaling the observed system so you can see if you have enough resources to handle the projected peak load, but it only works for resources you know about.

Capacity planning is like a pre-party checklist where you check if there are enough: appetizers, drinks, glasses, places to sit, etc. Assuming you know how many guests will show up and have a reasonable understanding of what they will consume, everything you checked should be fine. However, even if you miss something, you are still better off having planned for reasonable amounts of the key resources.

"What you fail to plan for, you are condemned to endure."
– Bob's Second Rule of Performance Work

Capacity planning starts by gathering key performance meters at a peak time on a reasonably busy day. Almost any day will do, as long as the system load is high enough to clearly differentiate it from the idle system load. Then ask the boss: "How much larger is the projected peak than what I have here?" Answers like: "2X" or "about 30% more" are the typical level of precision you get.

Now scale (multiply) the observed meters by the boss's answer to get the projected peak utilization.

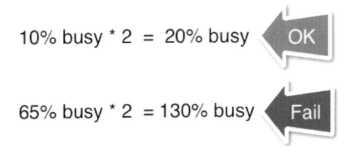

Often you will then find a resource, or two, that will be too busy at your projected peak. In that case, the load has to be handled by:

- Moving it to a faster machine
- Splitting it over several machines
- Reengineering the application for efficiency

In my experience, the application is rarely reengineered unless the inefficiency is egregious and the fix is easy and obvious. In most situations, people tend to value application stability more than the money they will spend to solve the problem with more hardware.

Capacity planning can be that simple, but there are a few more things you need to consider.

Even though you base your projections on one peak day, you should look at the data over a period of a few days to a few weeks. This gives you a clear picture where the usual daily peaks are and if there are things going on at odd times that you have to factor into any changes you propose.

Capacity planning can show you how busy key resources are at peak load, but it can't tell you about response time changes as the load increases. Even if you had perfect metering, doing the math would be a staggering challenge and, even, then you'd be gambling the business on reams of calculations. I'm very sure the CIO looking at all this complex math would feel very uneasy betting his or her job on these calculations.

Many key resources do not have a utilization meter, and the ones that do can lie to you. These resources take a little more work and creativity to capacity plan for, but this is completely doable.

Capacity planning is a good first effort at dealing with a future peak load. It can be done in a few days, presented in a few slides and prepared with few additional costs or risks. If you need more confidence in your plan, or you need to hold the response time down to a reasonable level, or if the future you are planning for includes significant changes to the transaction mix or vital systems, then you need to do either Load Testing or Modeling. They sound a little scary but, as Douglas Addams once wrote, "Don't Panic."

Load Testing

Load testing is the art of creating artificially generated work that mimics the real work generated by the real users. The overall load starts off low and then increases in stages to the point where you achieved your goal or you fail because some resource has hit a limit and has become a bottleneck. When that happens, throughput stops increasing, response times climb to an unacceptably painful place and things break.

Load tests depend on good performance monitoring to keep an eye on critical system resources as the load builds. For any test you need to know how much work you are sending into the system, the throughput and response time for the completed work, and how the system resources are responding under that load. Let's look at an example:

Work Goal	Work Achieved	Response Time	CPU Busy	Disk Busy
10 /sec	10 /sec	0.8 sec	10%	4%
50/sec	50 / sec	1.0 sec	42%	18%
250/sec	**118 /sec**	**18.3 sec**	**97%**	43%

In the above load test our goal rate was 250 transactions/sec. The system worked fine at 50/sec but bottlenecked at 118 transactions/sec with a very high response time, and the CPU clearly exhausted at 97% busy. As we say in New England: *You can't get there from here.*

Now you can retest this system increasing the load in finer steps between 50 and 120 transactions/sec looking for the point at which the numbers start to become unacceptable.

For a load test to be really useful it must test the entire part of the transaction path that you care about. If your product is your website then you need to test from where your users are: all the way in and all the way back to where they live. If you (and your boss) only have responsibility for a small subset of the entire transaction path then that's all *you* really need to test. The three big keys to a successful load test are:

- Make the generated work look like what you expect during the projected peak load
- Design the test to test the whole transaction path
- Increase the load in stages, looking for the point where things go bad

Load testing can also use capacity planning tricks. If you only got half way to your goal before you hit a bottleneck, then every measured resource is going to be doing twice the work once you fix the current bottleneck. So take all the peak measurements and double them to get a good idea of what you are likely to run out of as you push the test to the goal load.

Load testing can also help you find where subsystems break, and isolate the effect of one transaction type. Imagine your workload is an even mix of **Red** and **Blue** transactions, but it is the **Blue** transactions that really exercise some key component of your computing world. Create a load test that sends in all **Blue** transactions and you can collect the data you need without the interference of the **Red** transactions.

Load testing can tell you many interesting things, but it can only give you data on the computing infrastructure you have now. To use a metaphor, running a race tells you about your current aerobic capacity, not the capacity you will have after six more months of training.

If you need to predict a future that is different from your present, then you need to model. To model, you are going to need the data you collected with performance monitoring and maybe some data from load tests.

Modeling

Modeling computer performance may be unfamiliar to you, but is should not be frightening. Everyday, in companies all over the world, regular people build simple models that answer important business questions.

Here are a few general truths about modeling that may surprise you:

- A simple, but very useful model, can be created with a piece of paper in just a few minutes.

- You can build amazing models with just a spreadsheet.

- A serious response time model for a big, commercial, multi-tier application takes 2-4 weeks of work to create.

- Your model doesn't have to be perfect, just good enough to answer the question(s) being asked.

- You don't need to model the detailed program logic or every possible transaction.

- You don't need a super computer, just a humble laptop, to build and run a model.

- Since any incoming workload and complex application infrastructure can be simulated, you save a ton of time and money on test hardware and load generation tools.

- Regular people, who are not math wizards, can create the full range of useful models. This isn't rocket science; it's bookkeeping.

When your boss asks you to predict future performance of some application, first see if you can do a simple capacity plan. If circumstances change so much that you lack confidence in that prediction, then try modeling. Examples of big changes that preclude simple capacity planning might be things like, large application or middleware changes or a big change in the incoming workload. Modeling is the only way to project the performance of an application in the design stage where there is no performance data to scale.

In performance work there are really only two possible situations. Either you can directly measure the performance of a live system under load, or you have to guess about a theoretical future situation. You must accept that:

- Any model is just a detailed guess.

- To some degree, your guess will be wrong.

- The farther out you predict, the less accuracy your model will have.

How accurate does a model need to be? The flip answer is: accurate enough. A useful answer is: accurate enough to answer your question with a reasonable margin of safety.

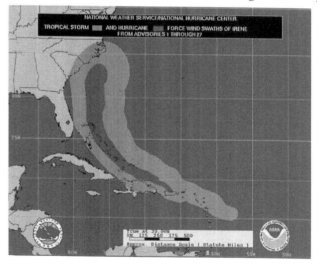

The above model of Hurricane Irene is accurate enough for anyone with a house on the Gulf of Mexico and it looks hopeful for Florida's Atlantic coast as well.

In a computer context, imagine your model shows that at peak load this server's CPU is 20% busy. It doesn't take a genius to understand that your model could be off by a lot and the server would still have plenty of CPU power left. The closer to the utilization limit (or the projected storm track), the more precise you have to make your model.

Unfortunately, the above model of Hurricane Irene, at that moment, could not see far enough into the future to predict the devastating flooding Irene would cause in my home state of Vermont. All models have limits.

If you respect these limits, modeling is doable, useful and has its place when you are asking questions about the future.

Right Tool For The Job

Watts = Volts * Amps

Chapter 3

USEFUL LAWS
AND THINGS I'VE
FOUND TO BE TRUE

Some things are true everywhere.

This chapter gives you the keys to understanding all computer performance problems and provides an important foundation for the next four chapters.

Ideas, Tools, and Tricks

Regardless of what hardware you are using, what software you are running, or the demands placed upon you by management, these are the fundamental forces that will drive your performance work. Understanding these forces and working with them (as opposed to against them) is how you put the wind at your back and get important things done.

I've seen the ideas, tools, and tricks in this chapter work on four different continents, at a hundred different companies, on good code and bad. Many of these, I learned from other performance gurus. They worked for them, they worked for me, and so I believe, they will work for you too.

A couple of the things presented here will seem so obvious that they have a "Well duhh…" quality about them. That's okay. Just realize the people who've never faced these questions may be a bit unsure about what appears to be common sense. These laws have been well researched and are known to be true. You can use them with confidence.

Don't Panic

This chapter uses complex things such as queueing theory, and a few well-known laws from the field of Operations Research, like Little's Law. All that can sound scary to some people, but fear not; what I am presenting here only requires simple math and common sense.

I encourage you to read it all because there are ideas, terms and fundamental concepts I introduce here that are used throughout the book.

If you are gifted in the ways of mathematics and a stickler for detail, you will find I left all that detail out, ignored special cases, and do not show the deep math behind these ideas. Why? Because most people, including the author, can't do that math, and there many useful things that you can do without it. You don't have to be an expert on thermodynamics, combustion physics, and protein chemistry to barbecue a delicious hamburger.

I paid off my mortgage by doing useful, productive performance work with the ideas presented here. Many of these ideas are based on highly complex math that I will leave to other books. Here I will show how these powerful ideas can be used by anyone with grade school math.

The Abyss

At the Grand Canyon there are many places where you can walk right up to a cliff where, with one more step, you will fall hundreds of feet to your death. The closer you are to the edge of a cliff, the more precisely you need to know your location. In your campsite, a half-mile away, your exact location is not so life-critical. This is also true in performance work.

If the numbers show a resource will be 20-25% busy at peak, I would not spend more time getting a more precise version of that number. You could be off by a factor of two and the resource would most likely be fine at 40-50% busy. Obviously, the closer you are to some performance limit, the more careful you have to be with your calculations, models and predictions.

With any prediction of future behavior there will also be some error, some uncertainly. Some of this is your fault, some of it is the fault of the person who specified the peak load to plan for, and some of it is the fault of the users who didn't do exactly what was anticipated on that peak day.

When the boss says plan for a peak load that is two times the observed load, do what you are asked. Then, look to see if you are close to "the edge" of the performance cliff. If you are close to some limit, go back to the boss and show what you've found and ask: "How sure are you about your predicted peak load?"

I've seen many cases where, when shown how close to the edge a system would be at peak, the decision makers change their minds and give me a different number to plan for.

Sometimes that number is:

- Bigger because they want to buy a new stuff
- Smaller because they don't want to spend money
- Bigger to protect the budget for next year
- Smaller because they just got new growth projections
- Different than the last number because of the crisis they are dealing with at the moment you happened to ask

It your job is to advise, not decide. Present your data, give your best advice, and be at peace. A business decision weighs costs, risks, politics, and the art of what is possible.

The Brick Wall Of Busy

Nothing can be more than 100% busy. No matter how much your boss wants it to be so, there is no 110% to give. Furthermore, you are doing the wrong thing 99% of the time if you plan to use anything near 100% of any resource at peak load.

Response Time and Utilization

Response time is the total amount of time you waited for something you asked for. Here is an example:

Time	Action
00:00	You say: "Can I have a cookie?"
00:02	Mom takes a cookie from the jar.
00:04	Mom hands you the cookie.
00:05	You insert cookie and begin chewing.

As far as your taste buds were concerned, the response time for your cookie request was five-seconds. If Mom had been busy doing other things, then you would have had to wait and that would lengthen the response time.

Utilization is the technical term for "busy" and is typically expressed as a decimal fraction with a range between zero and one. A 45% busy resource has a utilization of 0.45.

As utilization goes up, the response time also tends to go up. There are powerful insights and useful guidance to be found in this relationship. To get there, I'm going to introduce a few more technical terms we'll use throughout the book to explain and predict how things work, back up, and slow down when things get busy.

Service Center and Service Time

A service center is where the work gets done. CPUs, processes, and disks are examples of service centers. To accomplish a given task, it is generally assumed that it takes a service center a fixed amount of time – the **service time**. In reality this assumption is usually false, but still very useful.

Service Center

The crafty people who designed your hardware and software typically put a few optimizations in the design. If you could meter every job going through a service center you'd find that the amount of time and effort to accomplish each "identical" job is somewhat variable. Having said this, it is still a useful abstraction to think about each identical task taking an identical amount of time to be serviced at the service center. Just as you don't require quantum mechanics to predict the flight path of a baseball, you can mostly ignore the individual variations and focus on the big picture.

Averaged over time, a service center can have a utilization from zero to one or, if you prefer, 0% to 100% busy.

You are always interested in the utilization averaged over a short period of time, i.e., seconds or minutes.

You are never interested in the instantaneous utilization (it is always 0 or 1) and are rarely interested in the utilization averaged over long periods (hours, days, etc.)

Only a fool would plan for a service center to be 100% busy, as there is no margin for error and the incoming work usually does not arrive at a convenient pace.

You can set the boundaries of a service center anywhere you like. A service center can be a simple process, or the entire computer, or an entire array of computers. For that matter a service center can be an oven. The service time for baking bread = 30 minutes at 350°F. A service center is where work gets done, and you get to define the boundaries.

Arrivals and Throughput
Work arrives at a service center and, when processing is complete, it exits. The work is composed of discrete things to do that might be called transactions, jobs, packets, tasks, or IO's, depending on the context.

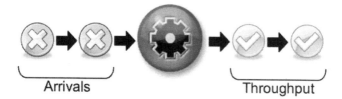

The rate at which tasks arrive at the service center is the arrival rate. The rate at which tasks exit a service center is called the throughput. In performance work, most of the time these values are measured over a period of a second or a minute and occasionally over a longer period of up to an hour.

To stay out of trouble, be sure that you don't confuse these terms and keep your units of time straight. Arrivals are not the same as throughput, as anyone knows whose ever been stuck in a long airport security line. If you accidentally mix "per second" and "per minute" values in some calculation, then badness will ensue. Try not to do that.

Wait Time

Unless you are reading this in a post-apocalyptic world where you are the only survivor, there will be times when tasks arrive at a faster rate than the service center can process them. Any task that arrives while the service center is busy has to wait before it can be serviced. The busier the service center is, the higher the likelihood that new jobs will have to wait.

The upper limit on wait time is controlled by two things: the maximum number of simultaneous arrivals and the service time. If ten tasks arrive simultaneously at an idle service center where the service time is 10 milliseconds, then the first task gets in with zero wait time, the last job will wait for 90 milliseconds. The average wait time for all these tasks is:

$$45ms = (0+10+20+30+40+50+60+70+80+90) / 10$$

The overall response time is what most people care about. It is the average amount of time it takes for a job (a.k.a. request, transaction, , etc.) to make it through the service center and (typically) back to the user. For any given service center:

$$ResponseTime = WaitTime + ServiceTime$$

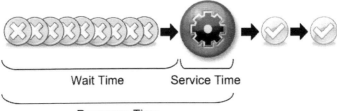

Wait Time   Service Time

Response Time

Finding What You Don't Have

Now that we have a few terms defined, let's look at some tools and rules that will help you find useful information, spot errors, and give you key insights about how systems behave when they get busy.

Finding Wait Time and Service Time

As you'll see shortly, the wait and the service time are wildly useful numbers to know, but the response time is the only number that most meters, if they provide that data at all, are likely to give you. So how do you dig out the wait and the service time if there are no meters for them?

The service time can be determined by metering the response time under a very light load when there are plenty of resources available. Specifically, when:

- Transactions are coming in slowly with no overlap
- There have been a few minutes of warm-up transactions
- The machines are almost idle

Under these conditions, the response time will equal the service time, as the wait time is approximately zero.

ServiceTime + WaitTime = ResponseTime

ServiceTime + 0 = ResponseTime

ServiceTime = ResponseTime

The wait time can be calculated under any load by simply subtracting the average service time from the average response time. This is a useful calculation to do as it shows you how much better things could be if all the wait time was cleared up. Performance work, at some level, is all about time and money. If you know the wait time, you can show how much time a customer might save if your company spent the money to fix the problem(s) you've discovered.

Finding the Maximum Throughput

If you know the service time, you can find the maximum throughput because:

$$MaxThroughput \leq 1 / AverageServiceTime$$

A service center with an average service time of 0.05 seconds has a maximum throughput of: $1 / 0.05 = 20$ per second.

CAUTION: With this calculation you have to be a bit careful when you have a broadly defined service center. For example, a Google search with the word "cat" returned after 0.25 seconds. This value was reasonably constant when tested very early in the morning on a weekend so we can assume that the utilization of the Google servers is fairly low. Using the above formula, we can scientifically show that the maximum throughput for Google is four searches per second. Clearly that is not right. So, is this rule wrong? No, it was just used in the wrong place. Google has a massively parallel architecture, and so we are not looking at just one service center. Here we got a reasonable Average Service Time, did the calculation, and came up with a Max Throughput number that made no sense. With all these tools the most important things you bring to the party are common sense and a skeptical eye.

Finding The Mean Number of Jobs In The System

Little's Law shows the fixed relationship between three things: the mean number of jobs in the system that are either waiting or being serviced, the mean response time, and the mean throughput. If you know two of these three things you can figure out the third. This can be useful when doing a quick validation of metered data and for checking the soundness of proposals and plans.

Suppose you are capacity planning for an application that (as either a licensing or a configuration restriction) has an upper limit on the number of concurrent requests being processed, and you need to know how close you are to that limit according to Little's Law:

MeanNumberInSystem =
MeanResponseTime * MeanThroughput

Imagine the application has a mean response time of 0.2 seconds and a throughput measured at 50/second. The mean (average) number in the system is: 10 = 0.2 * 50

Finding The Average Response Time

Here we can also use Little's Law when applications thoughtlessly do not have any easy way to meter response time. If all you can find is the mean number in the system and the throughput, you can rearrange the equation to find the response time info you need like so:

MeanResponseTime =
MeanNumberInSystem / MeanThroughput

Now we'll look at the same application with different meters. Here we have a meter (like queue depth) that tells us the number of jobs waiting to be serviced. There are nine jobs in the queue and one being processed, so there is an average of ten jobs in the system. Another meter shows a mean throughput of 50 per second. You can calculate the mean response time as: 0.2 seconds = 10 / 50 per second

When exploring Little's law and learning to trust it, be aware of the common newbie mistakes of using arrivals when throughput is called for and not keeping the units of your measurements the same.

Also Little's law expects the system to be in a steady state during the measurements, with no surges or drop-offs in demand, and that all the jobs are uniform in size. Given that in real life applications these restrictions are never fully met, Little's Law is mostly useful for reality checking (do the meters make sense) and ballpark estimations of missing performance numbers.

Finding How Busy a Resource Is

The Utilization Law, using the same definitions, limits, and restrictions of Little's Law, allows us to estimate the utilization of a service center if you only know the service time and the mean throughput like so:

MeanUtilization = ServiceTime * MeanThroughput

This is really helpful when you are studying a complex service center, such as a key process in the transaction path, that burns a little CPU, does some disk I/O, and communicates with other processes. Typically processes do not have a utilization meter that encompasses all these activities. You can usually know the CPU utilization of a process, but a process can be bottlenecked long before it hits 100% CPU utilization.

You could, for example, monitor a process as it experienced a normal workload with a network sniffer. By picking through a couple of minutes worth of data, you could gauge the service time and mean throughput of the process and that would allow you to calculate its overall utilization. With a utilization and mean throughput number, you could then gauge how much more headroom this process has like so:

HeadRoom = 1 − (ServiceTime * MeanThroughput)

The key thing to remember here is that the service time of the process is not likely to improve as the load increases. Therefore, the max throughput number you generate is likely to be the most optimistic case.

Finding The Service Time a Different Way

The complex math of operations research that defines the Service Demand Law boils down to a simple idea. You can divide any utilization number the system gives you by the throughput rate to find the cost per transaction.

ServiceTime = MeanUtilization / Mean Throughput

For example: Imagine a system is processing 20 transactions

per second with an overall CPU utilization of 0.8 or 80% busy. At one transaction per second the CPU utilization would be: .8/20= 0.04 or about 4% busy. If that system can provide 4000 milliseconds of CPU service per second (thanks to its four CPUs) then four percent of 4000 milliseconds = 160 milliseconds of CPU per transaction.

The Service Demand Law can be useful when you need to do a capacity plan where part of the overall transaction load is being moved to another system. It is easier to scale a number like 160 milliseconds CPU than a more complex number like 4% CPU busy.

Finding The Poor Man's Transaction Meter

Operations research also gives us the Forced Flow Law, which confirms a useful, common sense insight that all the parts of the transaction path have to service the transactions as they flow through them. If you can meter that service at any point you can know a lot about the other parts of the system.

Most applications have no throughput metering at all or only tell you their throughput on some useless time scale like daily or weekly. It is important to know the average throughput of work at the same time you are sampling the system performance meters. What the Forced Flow Law gives us is a way to build a poor man's transaction meter. All you have to do is find one thing you can easily meter that has a stable relationship with the amount of work the system is doing and, Voila, you know the transaction rate.

For example, suppose your system only reported the throughput as a daily value, and you noticed a stable relationship between the daily transaction rate and meter X over several days, like so:

Meter X Per Day	Transactions Per Day
23,045	10,000
46,073	20,000
2315	1,000 (slow day)

Here it is clear that for every transaction, meter X increments by 2.3 ≈ 23,045 /10,000. The relationship doesn't have to be perfect because the metering is rarely perfectly aligned, and there is always noise in any data you collect. You don't have to understand the details of the relationship just as you don't have to understand daffodil biology to know that when they are blooming in your yard it is most likely spring.

Now you can collect meter X over any interval you like, divide its value by 2.3, and get the transactions per interval.

Seeing Is Believing

You will often find yourself confronted with *massive amounts* of numeric data. Since the human mind is optimized to find patterns visually, not to comprehend thousands of numbers at a time, the data is often best understood in a chart.

Always convert the data-diarrhea the meters give you into graphical form. This is also true when presenting your data. Put up a slide full of numbers and you'll lose your audience in seconds.

The Hidden Truth

When looking at summarized data, you can miss opportunities to spot the problem, understand its severity and find its root cause.

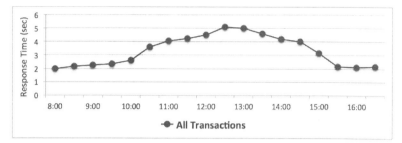

All Transactions

The graph above shows the average response time for all transactions combined into one line. The graph below shows the same data broken out for the major transaction types. With this new data you are drawn to the Search transaction and its transaction path as you look for the cause of the problem.

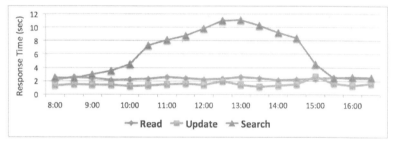

Read — Update — Search

Be sure you understand what has been averaged into each data point. Above we see one data point for each half hour. Is that the average of all transactions during that time, or is it a shorter sample taken every 30 minutes? The answer is not too important here, because the problem persists for hours. When you are chasing an intermittent or short duration problem, you need to know if the meters were sampling during the problem and how much data was averaged into each point as you'll see in Chapter 4.

Extraordinary claims

When presenting your conclusions keep in mind this quote by Marcello Truzzi: "An extraordinary claim requires extraordinary proof." If your conclusions are controversial, disruptive, or very expensive to fix, then you will need overwhelming proof because there will be strong resistance to your findings. This is the very human side of performance work.

Throughput and Workload

Let's look at a throughput graph that you'll most likely see over and over in the performance data you collect.

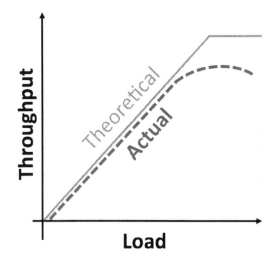

On an idle system, when work shows up, it gets processed right away and exits. ResponseTime = ServiceTime. So early on, as the workload starts to build for the day, the arrival rate of work equals the throughput. This happy circumstance continues until some part of the transaction path can no longer keep up with the arriving work. Now the following things start happening:

- Wait time starts to build
- Response Time starts to build (it includes Wait time)
- The throughput stops matching the arrival rate

At some point the throughput stops going up and can get worse as algorithms are pushed beyond their design limits and become dysfunctional.

When you see the throughput of the system flatten out like this, somewhere in the transaction path a resource is 100% busy. This graph is a cry for help. Learn to recognize it.

Law of The Minimum

Long before computers, two chemists named Sprengel and Liebig were working in the area of agricultural chemistry. Among their many accomplishments, Sprengel pioneered and Liebig popularized the Law of the Minimum, which states that growth is limited by the least available resource.

If a plant is starving for nitrogen, then only additional nitrogen will get things growing again. Everything else you give it doesn't help. Oddly enough the Law of the Minimum applies to computers, too.

When doing capacity planning you study the current consumption of resources, project future consumption based on an increased workload, and then produce recommendations on how to handle the projected workload. If, for example, your projections show the system will be out of disk IO capacity, adding anything else but a disk won't help at all. Extra resources may help new transactions move through the system quicker, but all that really does is hurry them to the disk bottleneck, where they will find themselves at the end of a very long line of transactions waiting for (in this case) disk IO. If you screw up and add the wrong resource, the queue of waiting tasks at the least available resource will just get longer and there will be no positive effect on throughput or response time.

In the biological sciences too much of something (water, warmth, etc.) can kill you just as easily as too little. In computers, if you have too much of some resource (like memory, bandwidth, CPU, etc.) there is no negative effect on the overall capacity of the system to get things done. Every so often I run into people who believe the myth that a system has too much of a given resource and that somehow hurts performance. It takes considerable time to talk them out of this belief. Be patient with them.

In business, money is often the most limited resource. If the system has too much of some resource, you are wasting money. The trick is to always have just enough resources in place to handle the peak plus a bit more as a margin of safety. Any fool can do capacity planning with limitless money.

It's Always Something

If you do your work just right, and the company follows your sage advice to the letter, there will still be times when the system runs out of resources. Why? Because those rascally users have a mind of their own. Market forces change, competitors fail and their load shifts to you, parts of your computing world fail and the load shifts to the remaining machines, price changes skew the normal transaction mix, etc.

That is why, once you have completed the capacity plan for the next yearly peak, you don't spend the intervening eleven months on the golf course. Gather data all year. Recheck your capacity projections periodically. Look for new meters and double check old meters. See if management has changed its projected peak load. See if the transaction mix has changed. See how new hardware or software changes your projections. If you stay vigilant, change is still inevitable, but suffering can be optional.

The Hidden Bottleneck

When you run out of some resource, that resource becomes a **bottleneck**. All the transactions race through the system only to find a huge queue because of that resource limitation.

The double-necked hourglass illustration shows a bottleneck at point A. Beyond that bottleneck life is easy for the rest of the system as, no matter how many transactions arrive, the workload is throttled by the upstream bottleneck.

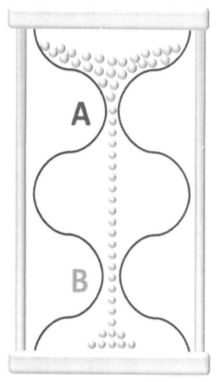

If you "fix" bottleneck A then performance will be really good for only about 45 milliseconds until that great load of transactions hits bottleneck B with a sickening "WHUMP!" The throughput of this system will hardly change at all, and you will have some explaining to do in the boardroom.

When capacity planning, it is important to explain this drawing to the decision makers so they comprehend how one bottleneck can hide a downstream bottleneck. It is also key for you to meter all the resources you can deplete, not just the one that is the obvious bottleneck.

The hourglass could easily have been drawn with many more bottlenecks, but I've never seen a performance problem where there were more than two bottlenecks that had to be cleared up to get the needed throughput. If you are working on the fourth bottleneck for this given problem, then perhaps you should spend some time thinking about a new career – because you are most likely deep in the weeds.

Queuing Theory

Queuing theory provides a way to predict the average delay at a service center when the arrival rate is greater than the throughput, or, according to Murphy's Law, whenever you are in a hurry. The calculations are complex, but luckily we can ignore the math and focus on the profound insights this branch of mathematics can bring to performance work.

As the utilization of a service center grows, it becomes more likely that a newly arriving job will have to wait because there are jobs ahead of it. The formula that describes this relationship is:

$$ResponseTime = ServiceTime / (1 - Utilization)$$

The real insight comes from looking at the graph of this function below, as the utilization is goes from 0% to 90%.

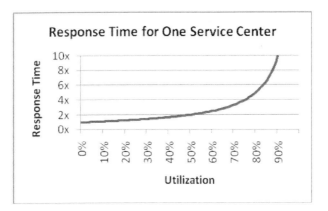

Notice that response time starts out as 1x at idle. At idle the response time always equals the service time as there is nothing to wait for.

Notice that the response time doubles when the service center gets to 50% utilization. At this point, sometimes the arriving jobs finds the service center idle, sometimes they find it with several jobs already waiting, but the effect on the average job is to double the response time as compared to an idle service center. The response time doubles to 4X when the service center is at 75% utilization and doubles again to 8x at around 87% utilization. Assuming you kept pushing more work at the service center, the response time doublings keep getting closer and closer (16x at 94% utilization, 32x at 97% utilization) as the curve turns skyward. All these doublings are created by the fact that the service center is busy, and thus there will often be many jobs waiting ahead of you in the queue.

Insight #1:
The slower the service center, the lower the maximum utilization you should plan for at peak load. The slowest computer resource is going to contribute the most to overall transaction response time increases. Unless you have a paper-tape reader as part of your transaction path, the slowest part of any computer in the early part of the twenty-first century is the rotating, mechanical magnetic disks. At the time of this writing, on an average machine, fetching a 64 bit word from memory was ~50,000x faster than getting it off disk.

The first doubling of response time comes at 50% busy and that is why conventional wisdom shoots for the spinning magnetic disks to be no more than 50% busy at peak load. Think about it this way, if the boss insists that you run the disk up to 90% busy then the average response time for a disk read will be about 10X slower than if the drive was idle. Ouch!

Insight #2:

It's very hard to use the last 15% of anything. As the service center gets close to 100% utilization the response time will get so bad for the average transaction that nobody will be having any fun. The graph below is exactly the same situation as the previous graph except this graph is plotted to 99% utilization. At 85% utilization the response time is about 7x and it just gets worse from there.

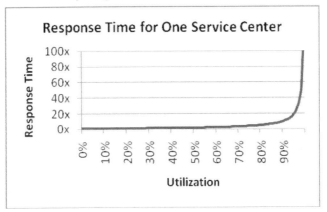

Insight #3:

The closer you are to the edge, the higher the price for being wrong. Imagine your plan called for a peak of 90% CPU utilization on the peak hour of your peak day but the users didn't read the plan. They worked the machine 10% harder than anticipated and drove the single CPU to 99% utilization. Your average response time for that service center was planned to be 10x, instead it is 100x. Ouch! This is a key reason that you want to build a safety cushion into any capacity plan.

Insight #4:

Response time increases are limited by the number that can wait. Mathematically, the queuing theory calculations predict that at 100% utilization you will see close to an infinite response time. That is clearly ridiculous in the real world as there are not an infinite number of users to send in work.

The max response time for any service center is limited by the total number of possible incoming requests. If, at worst case, there can only be 20 requests in need of service, then the maximum possible response time is 20x the service time. If you are the only process using a service center, no matter how much work you send it, there will be no increase in response time because you never have to wait for anyone ahead of you in line.

Insight #5:
Remember this is an average, not a maximum. If a single service center is at 75% utilization, then the average response time will be 4x the service time. Now a specific job might arrive when the service center is idle (no wait time) or it might arrive when there are dozens of jobs ahead of it to be processed (huge wait time).

The higher the utilization of the service center the more likely you are to see really ugly wait times and have trouble meeting your service level agreements. This is especially true if your service level agreements are written to specify that no transaction will take longer than X seconds.

Insight #6:
There is a human denial effect in multiple service centers. If there are multiple service centers that can handle the incoming work, then, as you push the utilization higher, the response time stays lower longer. Eventually the curve has to turn and when it does so the turn is sudden and sharp!

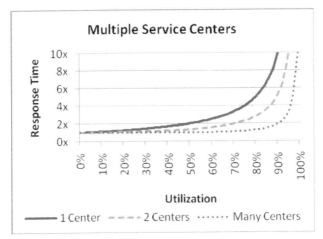

This effect makes sense if you think about buying groceries in a MegaMart. You are ready to check out and you look down the line of 10 cashiers and notice that seven of them are busy, three are free, so you go to the idle cashier. Even though the checkout service center is 70% busy overall, your wait time is zero, and therefore your response time is equal to the service time. Life is good.

On the other hand, if you have a system with eight available CPUs the response time will stay close to the service time as the CPU busy climbs to around 90%. At this point the response time curve turns upward violently. Add enough work to get the CPU to 95% busy, and the system becomes a world of bad response time pain. So, for resources with multiple service centers, you can run them hotter than single service center resources, but you have to be prepared to add capacity quickly or suffer horrendous jumps in response time. Most companies are much better at understanding real pain they are experiencing now, as opposed to future pain they may experience if they don't spend lots of money now.

"Most corporations only learn through pain."
– Bob's Third Rule of Performance Work

Insight #7:

Show small improvements in their best light. If you see some change that will make the system 10% more efficient, when is the best time to tell your boss about it? If you reveal your idea during the slow season when the system is 20% busy, that small efficiency improvement will hardly be noticeable. If you wait until a busy time of the year when your system is on the ugly part of the response time curve you will be a hero and be a shoo-in for a promotion. Of course, I'm kidding here. When you do find a silly waste of resources that can be easily fixed, take the time in your presentation to show the effect this small fix will have at the next seasonal peak.

Application Inertia

A famous Marx Brothers bit:

> Patient: "Doctor, every time I do this it hurts."
>
> Groucho: "Well then, don't do that!"

When idle, the application is ready to serve your every need. When busy, the application is the cause of 100% of all capacity problems because of the way it has to use resources to get the work done. Sometimes the programmers could have chosen a much more efficient way of getting things done. The trouble is that the decision makers often do not want to change the application because those changes introduce uncertainty, bugs, availability, and compatibility concerns.

If you find a bit of application brain damage, feel free to include it in your report as a possible solution, but be prepared to just throw more hardware at the problem. It is a rare shop that will make a non-trivial change to the application without resistance.

Resource Usage Tends to Scale Linearly

Once you have a trickle of work flowing through the system (which gets programs loaded into memory, buffers initialized and caches filled), it has been my experience that if you give a system X% more work to do, it will burn X% more resources doing that work. It's that simple. If the transaction load doubles, expect to burn twice the CPU, do twice the disk IO, etc.

There is often talk about algorithmic performance optimizations kicking in at higher load levels, in theory that sounds good. Sadly, most development projects are late, the pressure is high, and the good intentions of the programmers are often left on the drawing board. Once the application works, it ships, and the proposed optimizations are forgotten.

Performance Does Not Scale Linearly

Independent parallel processing is a wonderful thing. Imagine two service centers with their own resources doing their own thing and getting the work done. Now twice as much work is coming, so we add two more service centers. You'd expect the response time to stay the same and the throughput to double. Wouldn't that be nice?

The problem is that at some point in any application all roads lead to a place where key data has to be protected from simultaneous updates or a key resource is shared. At some point more resources don't help, and the throughput is limited. This is the bad news buried in Amdahl's Law – which it something you should read more about.

When All Hell Breaks Loose

At very high transaction levels many applications can suffer algorithmic breakdown when utterly swamped with work. For example, a simple list of active transactions works well under normal load when there are usually less than ten things on the list, but becomes a performance nightmare once there are 100,000 active transactions on the list. The sort algorithm used to maintain the list was not designed to handle that load.

This can happen when a source of incoming transactions loses connectivity to you and, while disconnected, it buffers up transactions to be processed later. When the problem is fixed, the transaction source typically sends the delayed transactions at a relentless pace, and your system is swamped until it chews though that backlog. Plans need to be made to take into account these tsunami-like events.

For example, I've seen this at banks processing ATM transactions, where normally the overall load changes gradually throughout the day. Now a subsidiary loses communication and then reconnects after a few hours. That subsidiary typically dumps all the stored ATM transactions into the system as fast as the comm lines will move them. Building in some buffering, so that all the pending transactions can't hit the system at once, can be a smart thing to do here.

Sometimes the tsunami-like load comes as part of disaster recovery, where all the load is suddenly sent to the remaining machine(s). Here you need to decide how much money you want to spend to make these rare events tolerable.

Firefighting Addiction

For those who firefight performance problems, there is tremendous satisfaction in their heroic efforts. There is an adrenalin rush and a freedom of action that stands in stark contrast to the boring calm of an ordinary day. They have to act quickly and decisively without the usual 500 meetings it takes to decide anything. It's fun, addictive and sadly I have seen many examples of key staff members who have become so addicted to the rush that they do this all the time. It seems like hardly a day, or a peak, can go by without their personal intervention.

However, I've noticed something about this firefighting; when I examine their efforts, in most cases, they are really not having that much of an impact on measures like throughput or response time. One person I worked with sat at his desk for the first half hour of market open and, with the dexterity of a master organist, adjusted the priorities of processes. He thought it made a big difference; so did everyone else. He was a big wheel at that company, but in this case, he was completely wasting his time.

If someone at your shop has a bad case of firefighting addiction, it is tough to wean them away from it because you (with proper performance analysis and capacity planning) are taking away one of their most "valuable" contributions to the organization. Expect resistance.

Please do not get me wrong, I love those people who have what it takes to come up with just the right fix at a critical moment and have the courage to save the day. Those moments should be rare. If those moments happen daily, then what is really needed is some serious performance work to get at the root of the problem.

Application Knowledge

Every time I visit a new company, the people who work there want to teach me how the system does its work. Depending on what level of detail freaks they are, this presentation can vary from a useful 15 minutes to endless hours of brain-withering, data diarrhea. Try to make the best of this by planning your escape route; just like in fire safety – every meeting should have at least two pre-planned exits. Ask the questions that you need answers to up front before you black out.

Don't get too bogged down with the 156 different transaction types, the coding style, or what fields are updated when an XYZ transaction happens. Essentially every computer application in existence boils down to this:

1. Bits come in

2. Bits are transformed in memory by the CPU

3. Some waiting may happen

4. Bits get read or written locally

5. Bits go out

Before you skip the presentation altogether, consider the waiting mentioned in Step 3 above. Computers are built from shared resources. It can be tricky to meter when there is competition for those resources, or when transactions have to wait for data from other systems. There is rarely a meter that directly measures the time spent waiting.

When key processes are waiting for something, the meters will usually show plenty of available computing resources, but the system won't process any more work. As the load increases, average response times will lengthen, queues will grow, and throughput will stop increasing.

While enduring the detailed application discussion, pay attention when you see all transaction paths converging. When all roads lead to Rome, you should at least be suspicious that Rome will be a bottleneck. Also pay close attention to when the transaction path needs something from the slowest part of the system.

What you really need to know is transaction flow and the bird's-eye view of what is going on. The work comes from the user, arrives at X, goes to Y, where a database lookup is done, and then the answer goes back to the user through X.

You might recall the Charlie Brown animated specials. Whenever the adults are talking all you hear is a trombone going: *Wahh, wah, wahh, wah, wahhhh*. When listening to people tell me about the fine detail of the inner-beauty of their application, that's mostly what I hear too. So don't panic if you don't know every little detail of an application. You can do spectacularly useful work knowing almost nothing about how a given process transforms the bits.

All Meters Are Bad

You need metering data to do any performance work but metering data never perfectly adds up, never aligns 100%, and typically contains many numbers that are meaningless to you. If you are a type-A detail-oriented person, this can drive you nuts. I urge you to relax just a little bit.

When comparing different meters that look at the same general thing, they might be sampling at different points in the operating system. They may be reporting different units – for example, a disk read can be reported in bytes, file records, disk blocks, logical IO, or physical IO. They may be counting directly, or sampling indirectly, the values they are reporting.

Keep the big picture in mind. If meter A shows the CPU at 85% busy and meter B shows it at 84% busy, that's close enough. If meters that should agree differ by more than 10%, and that 10% is significant to your work, then try to solve that mystery as that will teach you new things about the meters.

Also, gentle reader, there is a non-zero probability that the meters might just be wrong. Just about the last thing that gets added into any system or application are performance meters. Mostly they are added in a hurry, to solve a problem, and most of their output might be utterly useless to anyone who doesn't work in the vendor's engineering department. Typically they are not part of the vendor's quality assurance (QA) work and so, unless someone notices, they can start telling lies as the years pass. They can also lie due to changes in technology over time. For example, in 1800 you might meter the utilization of a road by metering the horses that pass by per hour. That meter might still be around in 2012 and working perfectly, but will give the erroneous impression that the metered stretch of road has a rush hour utilization of zero.

Bad Meters Can Be Very Useful

Every so often you find a meter that you don't understand, but its output tracks some key metric nicely. For example, many businesses know the number of transactions they did yesterday, but have no idea how many happened in the last five minutes. So you find an odd meter that you can sample frequently: Disinbipulations = 3204 and you notice that the meter always tracts the daily transaction count nearly perfectly and the rate of change seems to track well with the other meters (like CPU) that show transaction load indirectly. This is a good thing to find because you now have a meter for the actual workload on the system.

The Perils of Serving Undercooked Ideas

Once you begin to work on a problem, people will almost immediately ask you your opinion on the cause of the problem and lots of questions that boil down to: "Will we be OK?" Nobody wants to wait. I can't blame them.

Reporting early results, before you've double-checked your work, is the road to disaster. You wouldn't give a hungry guest raw chicken; don't give hungry coworkers your raw, unchecked, conclusions.

Almost every time I have let someone wheedle an unchecked conclusion out of me it has turned out poorly. Doing this will erode organizational trust in your work as usually your conclusions change as you get more data. All they will remember is that at first you got it wrong. When relentlessly pressed, give them a juicy bit of observable data (example: We are seeing 4x the normal load.), but keep your conclusions to yourself.

Third Party Meters

May I humbly suggest that you beware the lovely entrapments of fancy-schmancy third-party performance meters. Oh the salesperson's voice will be buttery-smooth, and the multi-colored charts will call to you but, before you buy, consider these things:

- Can you find out the name of the low level meter that is the source of this beautiful graphic? If you can't, then the only people you can discuss this with are other users of this tool. Most likely the people in support (or the external vendor wizards) have never seen this tool and will ask for the basic operating system meters instead. This can make for an awkward and slow conversation in a time of a performance crisis.

- Is it clear when the displayed value was sampled and what the sample rate was? If not, you know almost nothing about that number.

- Does the package only display graphic data? Beautiful graphs are nice, but often you need the raw data in a spreadsheet for further analysis or presentation graphs.

- Can you incorporate application-specific workload information into that tool so you can see the workload and the performance data together?

- How many layers of software are between you and the raw performance data? Each layer increases the risk that the data you are looking at is wrong. I've visited many customers who were working with beautifully presented bad data due to a bug, and they had no idea.

- Is the collected data being archived in an "open" way so that, with a minimum of fuss, the data can be explored with other tools?

Please don't get me wrong. The best of these packages can be of great help, but some are all flash with little substance.

Use Your Common Sense With Meters

As you work with the meters I urge you to always take your best guess at what the meters will report before you look at the results. Once you look at all your results, always check to see if they are internally consistent.

If you just blindly accept what the meters tell you, then all manner of errors can creep into your world, and worse, you will have no clue when they do. If you expect to see 500 reads and you see (20 or 5000) then that is a mystery that needs to be solved. Your test could have crashed early; someone else could be on the machine without your knowledge; or, as I've seen in the past, something as simple as an automated backup kicks in and messes up your work. Your data has to make sense to you and be internally consistent.

If you have no expectations about the results of your metering and how these meters relate to each other and the transaction load, then someday you'll take bad raw data, then distill it into a beautiful (but meaningless) report, and give a bogus presentation that might just end up hurting the company and ending your career.

Trustworthiness

All of your efforts will be meaningless and wasted if the boss doesn't trust you, the quality of your work, and the results you've generated. They bet their job, and to some extent the future of the company, on your work. To succeed you should be honest and trustworthy as a person, and you need to:

- Check your work carefully every time as even small errors erodes confidence in your work.

- Never allow yourself to be forced into lying about the numbers as you present your way up the power chain to more and more senior management.

"If they don't trust you, your results are worthless."
 – Bob's Fourth Rule of Performance Work

How To Get Help

Performance work is a team sport. You can do it alone, but it is no fun and unnecessarily difficult. It is ten times easier to ask the right person for the data you need rather than trying to get it yourself. Here are a few techniques that have worked well for me over the years.

To get help, you need to be worthy of help. Start by being helpful to others before you need them. Give them access to your performance data. When possible, answer their questions with a minimum of fuss. When doing this, ask for nothing in return. If there is even a hint of Quid Pro Quo in your mind, then the smarmy stench of entrapment will negate all your good efforts.

When I need to ask an expert for some information, I like to help them look smart by letting them know what I want before I show up. This gives them a chance to prepare and I tend to get higher quality data out of them.

When looking for access, or a key piece of information, never take "no" from someone who can't give you a "yes". People often will say "no" with authority when they are unsure if they are allowed give you access. People often say "it's impossible" rather than admit they don't know how to get what you need.

Your crisis is not their crisis. Give people time to do what you need. You are much more likely to face rejection if you ask "Can I have your help right now?" than if you ask "When do you have time to help me?"

Getting An Answer From a Group

The best way to get an opinion from a group is with the Delphi technique.

- Ask multiple experts for their opinion privately.
- Consolidate those opinions removing the names.
- Feed the consolidated opinions back to the experts.
- Repeat and watch their thoughts converge.

I've found this particularly valuable when doing capacity planning and I am looking for the estimated size of the next annual peak.

Give Experts Occasional Privacy

If you have experts from the vendor come in to work a problem, it can be tempting to hang around them all the time to learn new things. However, it is in your own best interest to periodically give them a chance to confer privately and give them a private space to talk to the their home office experts.

Why? Out of your earshot they can confer frankly about your problem and hopefully come up with better solutions by:

- Talking freely to each other about what they do and don't know about your situation.

- Brainstorming possible next steps without worrying they look like idiots in front of you.

- Speaking candidly to their home office technical wizards about what they've observed, what they don't know, and their current theory as to the root of your problem.

Put yourself in their shoes. If you had to fix a big problem at a key customer, wouldn't you want some privacy as you sought advice, searched for answers, and evaluated possible solutions?

Chapter 4

PERFORMANCE MONITORING

"You can observe a lot by just watching." - Yogi Berra

This chapter focuses on how to meter and how to get the most out of your metering data.

About Performance Monitoring...

Companies assemble collections of technology to do work and they are very interested in getting that work done in a timely manner. All that technology gives out clues as to what it is doing and how hard it is working in the meters. When that technology can't keep up with the work, then everyone is interested in where the delay is happening.

There are always meters available and some of them are

actually useful. Meters are the raw materials of performance work. However, gathering huge amounts of metering data without any purpose is not science, it's hoarding.

There is no way to write a book that tells you to use this vendor specific meter, that particular way. The performance problems you face are too varied and the technology you work with is so diverse that writing an all-encompassing book is impossible. If the book was somehow created, it would be almost instantly out of date as the march of new versions of the technology is relentless. Imagine writing a book on operating motorized vehicles that had to explain the specific details of every make and model of car, bus, plane, train, lawnmower, backhoe, tractor, F1 race car and spaceship and how they should be controlled.

So, what to do? Here we will focus on:

- Fundamentals of Performance Metering
- Common mistakes and how to avoid them
- How to meter for different kinds of performance situations

The Question Drives The Search

The question you need answered drives your decision as to what to meter, what to ignore, and how you analyze the data. Always begin with the question you are trying to answer. Use it to figure out if you have the data you need, or if you have to explore further.

However, you need to keep the big picture in mind as well. You are the Grand Poobah of performance. Some days you have short-term performance problems to solve, other days seasonal capacity planning to do. Different jobs require different data. Collect some meters all the time and do some specialized metering for the questions or problems that pop up.

History Repeating

The worst pain comes from falling in the same hole twice. When you do the work to solve a performance problem, it is often a good idea to add something to keep an eye on that problem in your ongoing, always-running set of meters.

Also, it is often the case that what caused the previous performance problem is the first thing blamed for the next one. Every minute spent working on the wrong problem is wasted time and lost opportunity. Having that extra meter running can help you quickly determine if the same old problem is back, or there is a new mystery to solve.

What You Need to Know About Any Meter

For any meter you collect you need to know four things about it or it tells you almost nothing. Imagine you get a piece of data that states: **The application did 3000 writes.** Here are the things you don't know about it.

1. The Time The Meter Was Taken

First and foremost, you need to know when the data was collected because no meter is an island. It is almost never the case that all possible metering data comes from one source. You'll have to dig into various sources and coordinate with other people. The way you link them together is time.

Since time is usually easy to collect and takes up very little space, I always try to record the time starting with the year and going down to the second. 2012-10-23 12:34:23. You may not need that precision for the current question, but someday you may need it to answer a different question.

Adding the time can tell you: **The application reported 3000 writes at 3:05:10PM EST on June 19, 2012.** You can now compare and contrast this data with all other data sources.

2. The Sample Length of The Meter

Any meter that gives you an averaged value has to average the results over a period of time. The most common averaged value is a utilization number.

The two graphs below show exactly the same data with the only difference being the sample length of the meter. In the chart below the data was averaged every minute. Notice the very impressive spike in utilization in the middle of the graph. During this spike this resource had little left to give.

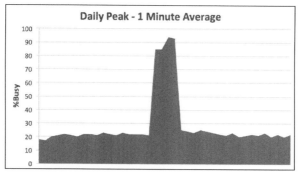

In the chart below the same data was averaged every 10-minutes. Notice that the spike almost disappears as the samples were taken at such times that part of the spike was averaged into different samples. Adjusting the sample length can dramatically change the story.

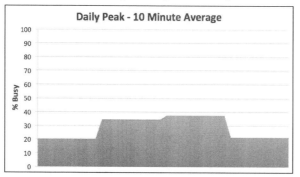

Some meters just report a count, and you've got to know when that count gets reset to zero or rolls over because the value is too big for the variable to hold. Some values start incrementing at system boot, some at process birth.

Some meters calculate the average periodically on their own schedule, and you just sample the current results when you ask for the data. For example, a key utilization meter is calculated once every 60 seconds and, no matter what is going on, the system reports exactly the same utilization figure for the entire 60 seconds. This may sound like a picky detail to you now, but when you need to understand what's happening in the first 30 seconds of market open, these little details matter.

Now, adding the sample length to what we already know about this meter, can tell you: **The application reported 3000 writes between 3:00-3:05:10PM EST on June 19, 2012.**

3. What Exactly Is Being Metered

As the old saying goes: "When you assume, you make an ass out of u and me." Here we have two undefined terms: application and writes.

An "application" is usually many processes that can be spread over many computers. So we need a little more precision here. Where did those 3000 writes come from? Just one process? All processes on a given system? All processes on all systems?

"Writes" can be measured in bytes, file records, database updates, disk blocks, etc. Some of these have much bigger performance impacts than others.

Even within a given metering tool, it is common to see the same word mean several different things in different places. Consistency is not a strong point in humans. So don't assume. Ask, investigate, test and double check until you know what these labels mean. The more precisely you understand what the meter measures, the more cool things you can do with it.

Now, adding the specifics about what is being metered can tell you: **All application processes on computer X reported 3000 blocks written to disk Y between 3:00-3:05:10PM EST on June 19, 2012.**

4. The Units Used in The Meter

Lastly, pay attention to units. When working with data from multiple sources it is really easy to confuse the units of speed (milliseconds, microseconds), size (bits vs. bytes), and throughput (things per second or minute) and end up with garbage. It is best to try to standardize your units and use the same ones in all calculations.

Since 5 minutes is 300 seconds, we can calculate the application was doing 10 writes/second = 3000 writes / 300 seconds.

So finally we can tell you that: **All application processes on computer X wrote an average of 10 blocks per second to disk Y between 3:00-3:05:10PM EST on June 19, 2012.**

Now we really know something about what's going on and have a value specified in a common unit we can compare and contrast with other data.

Lastly, here is a brief example illustrating how important correct use of units can be. I know of one company that had to give away about five million dollars worth of hardware on a fixed price bid due to a single metering mistake by the technical sales team where kilobytes were confused with megabytes. Ouch.

Begin Where You Are and Grow

To begin, just begin. Start with whatever metering is in place. Don't wait for perfect meters or perfect understanding of the meters. There will always be some mystery in the meters. That's OK. As Teddy Roosevelt once said: "Do what you can, with what you have, where you are."

Let the performance questions you face guide you as you learn to trust the meters you have and explore for new sources of information.

Collect Meters All The Time

To catch a performance problem you must have meters running when the problem happens. Some problems are expected (like load tests or seasonal peaks), but, if you want to solve the problems that pop up out of nowhere, you really need to have continuous monitoring.

So what meters do you collect for unexpected problems? The same ones you normally do. When any problem happens look for two things in your data:

Clues as to where the problem is

Clues as to where the problem is not

When a problem happens, the problem could be literally anywhere in your computing world and thus the problem space encompasses your entire computing world. As you look at your meters, many of them will show that a given part of your computing world is working well. That happy news tells you where not to search for the source of the problem. New performance people often focus on the bad news, like little kids playing soccer focus only on the ball.

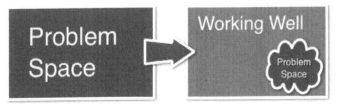

Paying attention to the good and bad news in the meters results in less wasted time and a more focused approach to finding the root cause of this problem as your metering data shrinks the problem space. Now you can add some metering to look for trouble in likely places and, if the problem happens again, repeat the advice above. Each time you'll have a smaller problem space to search.

Collect Meters At the Right Frequency

You often have choices to make about how frequently you want to collect metering information. There is no "right" answer to this because it depends on what you are doing.

The more frequently you meter, the higher the resolution is on your performance data (e.g. more pixels in the image) and the higher the cost of metering. For internal meters, the "cost" might be just a few CPU cycles and a little disk space. For external third party testing, the "cost" might be real money. Know the cost of your metering and find a good balance between cost and getting the data you need.

My rule of thumb is you need to meter at a frequency that will get you at least two or three good samples during the performance problem you are trying to study.

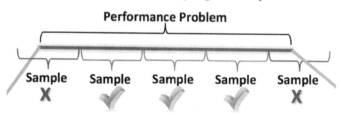

If you are studying long-term performance changes as the months, and years go by, you can meter at a very leisurely frequency. If your problem happens for an hour a day, sample every minute. If you are trying to catch a problem that usually lasts for a minute, I'd examine the meters every 10-15 seconds. Even one sample is better than nothing, but multiple samples make the case more convincing.

If your meters are used as inputs to some sort of alert system or dashboard, then you need to test frequently enough so the alarm is raised in a timely manner and there are multiple indications this is a real problem. Especially when some part of the transaction path goes over the Internet, you want multiple confirmations of a problem because sometimes bad things happen on the Internet that are random, short term, and totally out of your control.

If you are going to claim the sky is falling, you'd better have some pretty good evidence, as nothing erodes confidence in your work like raising a false alarm.

The frequency at which you choose to meter is also influenced by the sample length of the meter. Imagine a meter that reports the average utilization of resource X over the previous 60 seconds. If you sample that meter once every five minutes, then you are only collecting 12 samples per hour and have no data on resource X during 48 minutes (80%) of that hour. That may be just what you want as the problem you are studying typically lasts several hours once it starts so you'll get more than enough samples. However, if you are looking for the busiest minute to do some capacity planning with, then you only have a one-in-five chance of finding it.

Where this can lead to trouble is when you read too much into the data when you chart it. Below I plotted an hour's worth of data where I collected a meter with a one-minute sample length once every five minutes.

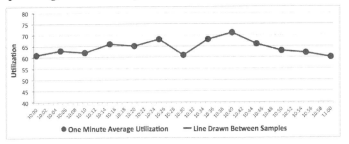

The dots on the line are the values the meter returned. They show the utilization of a resource averaged over a period of one minute. The line is just a line connecting the dots. In reality, we know nothing about what this resource was doing in the time between samples. However, our brain focuses on the line and believes the utilization smoothly changed from one dot to the next. Maybe it did, maybe it didn't. We don't know.

Performance data is usually noisier than the pretty graphs we draw, and the lines on those pretty graphs can fool us into thinking we know more than we do. When someone or some tool shows you a pretty graph be sure to ask what the sample frequency and sample length are if you really want to get something out of it.

Synchronize Your Meters

It can make your job simpler and your graphs look cleaner if the programs that collect the meters are synchronized to the top of the minute. This makes the data easier to combine and compare across systems.

Most metering programs or scripts are just a big loop of commands that gather metering data. At the bottom of that loop is usually something that waits until it is time to gather the next round of samples.

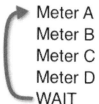

Meter A
Meter B
Meter C
Meter D
WAIT

Let's say you want these meters gathered once a minute. If you do the easy thing and just wait for 60 seconds, the meters drift in time because the meters themselves take time to run. At every iteration the meters would start a few seconds later in the minute. What you need to do at the bottom of the minute is wait until the beginning of the next minute. Then your meters will stay in sync with the top of the minute.

Confirm What You Are Metering

The only constant in this universe is change. Applications, operating systems, hardware, networks, and configurations can and do change on a regular basis.

It's easy to start the right meters on the wrong system. It's easy to miss an upgrade or a configuration change. Before any meter-gathering program settles down into its main metering loop, it should gather some basic data about where it is and what else is there. Gather things like:

- System name and network address
- System hardware CPU, memory, disk, etc.
- Operating System release and configuration info
- List of processes running
- Application configuration info

Most of the time this data is ignored, but when weird things happen, or results suddenly stop making sense, this data can be a valuable set of clues as to what changed.

Collect Workload Data With The Meters

Many things in your computing world, if properly asked, will give you some idea of how hard it is working. That's nice, but to make sense out of all that data, you need to know the workload the system is under. With workload data you see the meters with fresh eyes, as now you can evaluate how the system is responding to that workload and, with proper capacity planning or modeling, how the system will respond to a future peak workload.

To find or create a workload meter you and your coworkers have to agree on what the workload is and how to measure it. This will take some time as you've got to choose the transactions that will represent your workload from the many unique transactions users send in. Every company will settle on a different scheme and there is no perfect solution. Here are a few common ones I've encountered:

- Treat all incoming transactions the same. Simply count them and you have your workload number.

- Notice the vast majority of your incoming transactions do a similar thing, so count them as your workload number and ignore the others.

- Only count the transaction that was at the center of your last performance catastrophe as your workload. This may be an unwise choice as always swinging to hit the previous pitch you missed will not improve your batting average.

- Use the amount of money flowing into the company as the transaction meter. At $10K/min the CPU is 35% busy.

Whatever you decide to do will work fine as long as it passes the following simple test: Changes in workload should show proportional changes in the meters of key resources. What you are looking for is data like you see below.

Clearly as the measured workload increases the utilization of Resource X follows along with it. It is just fine that the lines don't perfectly overlap. They never will. It is the overall shape that is important. You are looking for these values to move in synchrony – workload changes cause a proportional change in utilization. Now, let's look at Resource Y below.

Resource Y is not experiencing any changes in utilization as the workload changes. This resource is not part of the transaction path for this workload. If it is supposed to be, perhaps you accidentally metered the wrong resource, or the right resource on the wrong system. I've made both of those mistakes.

Now, let's look at Resource Z below.

The utilization of Resource Z mostly tracks the workload meter (they rise and fall together) except for about an hour starting at 19:49 and ending at 20:39. Here you need to use some common sense, as either:

- The utilization spike could have been caused by something not related to the normal workload like a backup, or a software upgrade, or just the side effect of hitting some bug. In that case you can ignore the spike as you evaluate this workload meter.

- The utilization spike showed a dramatic increase in the workload, but your proposed workload meter did not see it. If your proposed workload meter missed a dramatic and sustained increase like we see here, then you need to search for a better workload meter.

Once you've decided what will serve as the workload meter, how do you get the data you need? It would be lovely if the application gave you an easy-to-access meter for that, but that rarely happens. Usually, you have to look in odd places. If XYZ transactions are going to be your workload indicator, then you need to find some part of the XYZ transaction path where you can find something to meter that uniquely serves that transaction. Here are some of the things I've done in the past to ferret out this key information:

- For every XYZ transaction, process Q does two reads to a given file. Take the number of reads in the last interval and divide them by two to get the transaction rate.

- For every 500 XYZ transactions, process Q burns one second of CPU. Take the number of CPU seconds consumed during the interval and multiply it by 500 to get the transaction rate.

- For every XYZ transaction file Z grows by 1200 bytes. Take the change in the file size during the interval and divide that by 1200 to get the transaction rate.

- For every XYZ transaction two packets are sent. Divide the packet count by two to get the transaction rate.

This list goes on, but the basic trick remains the same:

- First find some meter that closely follows the type of transaction you want to use as a workload meter.

- Then figure out how to adjust it mathematically so you get a transaction count.

That mathematical adjustment usually requires you to get multiple days worth of data and then, using whatever data you can get on your transaction, come up with the appropriate adjustment.

Reasonable people can argue that it is impossible to summarize a complex workload into one number. That may be true, but you can still do wildly useful things if you find a workload meter that approximately tracks the utilization of key components nicely. Every evening on the news they quote a major stock index (like the DOW, the FTSE, or the Nikkei) and we find that a useful gauge of the overall economy. When selecting the workload, don't go for perfect, go for close enough.

Collect Response Time Data

The whole reason companies build applications is to handle the work with reasonable response times. Users, and especially customers, do not tolerate long or highly variable response times well.

There are no response time meters in the systems, or other technology, that your computing world is built out of because the builders of that equipment don't know how you define a transaction. You are going to have to select the transactions you care about and build (or buy) response time meters for yourself. To do that, consider the following...

Selecting The Transactions You Care About

Clearly, the transaction(s) you use to define the overall workload on the system are leading contenders to meter for response time changes. You might also want to get some response time data on the transactions that bring the most money into your company. Imagine the SHOP transaction is 98% of your computing workload, but the BUY transaction brings in 100% of the money. For different reasons, I'd follow both of those transactions carefully.

Humans have a strong desire to avoid pain. If the last big performance disaster at your company (or at a competitor) was a response time problem of a particular type of transaction, I'd follow those carefully as well.

Meter Internal Response Time

Usually, you only have control over some of the computers that the transactions you process flow though. In the example below, system B is your responsibility and you are very interested in how responsive it is.

Understanding the internal response time (when A gives you work, how rapidly do you deliver the response) helps you in three ways by giving you an alibi, an insight, and a head start.

1. **Alibi**: When users are having response time problems, if you can show the response times are fine within your world, then the problem lies elsewhere.

2. **Insight**: If you see response times increasing internally, but there is nothing very interesting showing up in any of the performance meters you currently collect, then you have an undiscovered problem and you need to do some more exploring.

3. **Head start**: Sometimes response time problems take a while (hours, days, or even weeks) to be noticed and reported back to you or your boss. If you are paying attention to your internal response time meters, and the problem is located in your world, then you can be already working to find and fix the root cause of the problem when the boss knocks on your door.

Meter End User Response Time

It is also a good thing to test the response time as close to the user as possible. In this day and age that usually means testing outside your company across the Internet.

When testing across the Internet, the first thing you need to realize is that distance matters. If your users are spread out geographically, then those the farthest away will have the worse response times. The speed of light is not infinity, and the more distance you put between you and the customer the more delay they will experience.

You might reasonably point out that the few extra milliseconds don't matter on a human scale, but you need to remember that, at many levels, there are back and forth conversations going on like so:

Can I have GrandCanyon.jpg? >—>
                <—< Here is part #1, let me know when you get it.
Thanks, I got part #1. >—>
                <—< Here is part #2, let me know when you get it.
Thanks, I got part #2. >—>

Each back and forth pays the price of geographically induced delays. There was an interesting experiment the ACM did in 2009 where they repeatedly copied four gigabytes of data across the Internet, and the only thing they varied was the distance between the source and the destination computers. Below are their results that clearly show distance matters.

In testing response time close to the user, you also need to pay attention to using last mile connections that resemble

Distance	Network Latency	Time to Copy
<100 miles	1.6 ms	12 minutes
100-500 miles	16 ms	2.2 hours
3000 miles	48 ms	8.2 hours

what the users are using. There is a big difference in throughput, network latency, and error rates among dial-up, DSL, satellite, cable modems, fiber optic, and of course mobile cellular connections. You should look at your current user base and test your response time using those networks.

A small change in the amount of data you are sending to the user can have a big impact on response time if their network has a restricted throughput. For example, a user with a 40kilobit/second dial-up connection will see an additional second of response time when the amount of data sent increases by just 5000 bytes. Depending on the current conditions, mobile connections can also have surprisingly bad throughput and high error rates, which further slows things down.

Sometimes the big size increase of what you are delivering to the users happens to make some internal group happy, and no one notices as they all download the bits over the wicked-fast, low-latency corporate net. Then the change is rolled out to the general pubic and suffering ensues.

The Internet is a network of big, powerful networks that sometimes act like petulant little children who refuse to play nice with each other. Most of that trouble is intermittent, of short duration, and is completely outside of your control, but you do select a network  when you choose your company's ISP.

It can be a good thing to test response time using multiple ISPs from a given key geography. Imagine your customer service department starts getting complaints, but your internal meters all look good. Then you notice your response time tests that connect to the Internet via network X are all having troubles, but the tests connecting through ISP's using network Y and Z are all doing fine. Clearly, this is not your problem to fix, but it is wildly useful to know what is happening.

At this point you are probably thinking that all this testing sounds impossible to set up. Fear not, there are companies that have vast arrays of test machines all over the world and do this testing and provide detailed results to you as their business. When selecting a company to do this testing be sure that they can test:

1. From where your users are
2. The types of last mile connections your users use
3. The major ISPs your users use
4. From inside your company (extra credit)

Collect Error Data

XKCD.COM

Errors, even little ones, can be performance killers. Collect every meter you can find that tracks something unfortunate. Over time investigate what they meters are telling you.

- What causes this problem?
- Why is this problem happening?
- How does the system work around this problem?

The errors that most affect response time and throughput tend to be "timeout" errors, where something waited and waited and finally gave up. Big problems with timeout errors tend to show up as suspiciously low utilization. There is work waiting, but key resources are less busy than normal.

Some errors are unavoidable. You will always see a few of them in the data. The key is to know what's normal. When monitoring errors, notice when there are a lot more errors than usual for a given transaction rate. Investigate that.

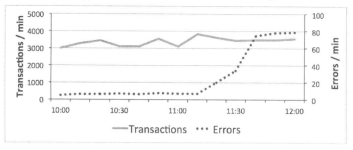

In the above graph the transaction rate is fairly steady, but just after 11:15 the error rate takes off. Don't panic. You need to keep a sense of scale here. At 12:00 there are about 3500 transactions per minute and just a little less than 80 errors per minute. So we are seeing approximately one error for every 43 transactions. You should still investigate this, especially if the response time increased at the same time. Given the low number of errors per transaction, this error is unlikely to be the cause of an overall response time problem, but it might be an interesting clue as to what's going on.

Collect Capacity Data

In computers, there are things to run out of, like free disk space, and limits that you can hit, like application licensing restrictions. These limits are not about how busy the thing is, but how full it is, and therefore, queuing theory doesn't really apply here. The performance of these things tends to be just fine until you run out of them; then things get bad in a hurry.

Keep an eye on what you can run out of, notice trends, and use that data to help you plan to bring new resources online at a convenient time of your choosing well before a crisis. Or, you can wait to run out, have a performance crisis, and spend a holiday weekend at work fixing things. It's your choice.

Switching Meters

There will come a time when new meters will replace the old meters. Sometimes this is your choice, and sometimes it is a corporate decision to standardize on a given tool. In any case, the key thing to do is run both metering systems in parallel so that you can see if the old and new meters tell the same story. Look for:

Differences in units - Are they both using the same unit for size (bytes) and speed (milliseconds)?

Differences in metering frequency - Are they both collecting and averaging over the same period?

Differences in terminology - Are they both using key terms in the same way? For example, in both metering tools is a write still the same kind of write and is it still based on the same low-level meter?

Difference in availability - Have you lost something you used to track in the old meters? What's new in the new meters?

If possible, run both the old and new meters for months before you shut down the old metering. This ensures you've given the new meters a good chance to show how they differ from the old meters and built up confidence that you can use the new meter data for all the different reports and other performance duties you have.

Confidence In A Small Sample

It is often the case that we just sample the response times of a few transactions rather than metering all of them. When sampling, how do you know you've sampled enough? If you make some change to the system, and the average response time falls from 10 seconds to 0.2 seconds, it doesn't take a rocket scientist to know that is a real improvement. However, if the before and after numbers are reasonably close, it's not as clear that that change was an improvement. We could have just gotten lucky in our sampling. So, how can we know anything without all the data?

Think about a bowl of jelly beans for a minute.

Imagine you blindly and randomly select and eat two jelly beans from that bowl. You find one is orange and one is strawberry. You could at this point state that the bowl contains 50% orange and 50% strawberry jelly beans, but you wouldn't be too confident about it. If the next ten randomly selected jelly beans confirmed the 50/50 ratio then your confidence would grow. However, to be absolutely certain of this ratio, you'd have to eat all the jelly beans in the bowl.

The same is true for any sampled data. The more sampled transactions you have, the more confident you are of your result. To be absolutely sure, you have to measure every transaction. But, how many samples is enough so you can be reasonably sure? For that we are going to have to use statistics, but please don't panic. We are going to use a couple of simple Excel functions to do the math. Let's work through an example.

Suppose you are comparing 100 samples of response time data before and after an upgrade to see if things are better or worse. Before the upgrade the average response time of 100 transactions was 4.5 seconds and after it was 4.1 seconds. To be sure a small difference is a real difference, you need to calculate the confidence interval. This is a four-step process:

1. Download/copy the individual response time data samples into a column of an Excel spreadsheet. For this example there 100 of them starting at cell A1 going through A100.

2. Use the **AVERAGE** function to find the average value (arithmetic mean) of all the samples. This function takes one argument, which is a range of cells containing the response times. For this example AVERAGE(A1:A100) equals 4.5.

3. Use the **STDEV** function to find the standard deviation of all of the samples. This function takes one argument, which is a range of cells containing the response times. For this example STDEV(A1:A100).

4. Use the **CONFIDENCE** function to find the confidence interval. The CONFIDENCE function takes three arguments:

   - Alpha - This is a number between zero and one that tells the function how confident we want to be. The confidence level equals 1 - Alpha. In other words, an Alpha of 0.02 asks for a 98 percent confidence level, which is what we want here.

   - StandardDeviation - This is the value returned by the STDEV function in step 3.

   - Count - This is the count of individual test results in our sample. In this example the count is 100.

The CONFIDENCE function returns a number: 0.51. This tells us that we can be 98% confident that the average response time of all transactions during the studied interval before the upgrade (not just the ones we sampled) is 4.50 seconds ± 0.51 seconds. In other words, we are 98% confident the average pre-upgrade response time is between 3.99 and 5.01 seconds.

Now, let's say we calculated the confidence interval for the after-the-upgrade data, and the calculations showed we are

98% confident that the actual average response time of all transactions during the studied interval (not just the ones we sampled) is 4.10 seconds ± 0.49 seconds.

So what does this all mean? If the confidence intervals overlap, there is no statistically significant improvement. As you can see below, they clearly overlap and, even though the after-the-upgrade response times numbers look better, statistics can offer no guarantee of any real improvement. The upgrade might have helped, but you can't prove it with the data you have to the level of confidence (98%) you want.

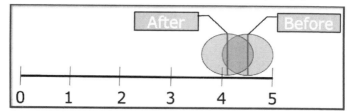

Now you might want to be absolutely 100% sure you are seeing an improvement. Statistics can't help you here because, to be 100% confident, you need to have response time data from ALL the transactions, not just a sample of them. If you have 100% of the data, you don't need statistics because you have 100% of the data. For most cases, a confidence level of 95% or 98% will do nicely.

This is the same calculation pollsters' do when they randomly call ~1000 people and, from that small sample, predict how the nation will vote. When these polls are talked about, they rarely quote the ALPHA or the confidence interval. If they did, the lead story of some future newscast might be:

The latest polls are 95% confident that candidate X is polling at 53% and candidate Y is at 48%. The margin of error is ± 5 points so there is no statistically measurable difference and thus we really have no idea who is winning.

How To Meter a Short Duration Problem

Some performance problems come and go within a minute or so. Depending on the industry, the company goals, and the expectations of the users, these problems are either a big deal or ignored with a yawn.

For short duration performance problems where you know when they will start (market open, 10pm backup, etc.) here are some tips for setting up special metering to catch them:

- Start your meters well before the problem happens and have them just sleep until a few minutes before the problem starts.

- Meter at a frequency that is at least ¼ of the expected duration of the event – this gives you multiple samples during the event.

- Let the meters run for a few minutes after the problem is usually over.

- Now you have meters collected before, during, and after the event. Compare and contrast them looking for what changed and what stayed the same during the event.

It is quite common for people to be suspicious that the new metering you are running is making the problem much worse. That's why it is a very good idea to have it running well before the anticipated start of the problem. There is some cause for this suspicion as a small typo can turn a "once per minute" meter into a "fast as you can" meter that burns CPU, fills disks, and locks data structures at a highly disruptive rate. Like a physician, your primary goal should be: First, do no harm.

If the problem happens without warning, then, if possible, identify something or some event that usually precedes the problem that you can "trigger on" to start the intensive metering. A trigger might be when the queue has over X things in it, or when something fails, or when something restarts, etc. Finding the trigger can sometime be frustrating, as correlation does not always mean causality. Keep searching the logs and any other meters you have.

Sometimes, all you have to go on is that it "happens in the morning" or "mostly on Mondays." Work with what you've got and meter during those times.

If the problem has no known trigger and seems to happen randomly, you'll have to intensively meter for it until it happens again. This will burn some system resources and give you a mountain of data to wade through. If this is a serious problem, then buckle up and do the work.

How To Meter For Capacity Planning

Capacity Planning is projecting your current situation into a somewhat busier future. To do this work you need to know what is being consumed under a relatively stable load, and then you scale that number to the projected load. So if some component of your computing world is 60% busy under the current load, it most likely will be 120% busy (and thus a serious bottleneck) under 2X the current load.

To meter for capacity planning you should collect data from every part of your computing world that shows:
- The current workload (transaction rate)
- How busy it is (utilization)
- How full it is (size, configuration or capacity limits)

Essentially you are looking to see how close you are to hitting any limit to growth, no matter how insignificant. Why? See the Law of The Minimum in chapter three.

If there are well understood and closely watched workload meters for your system (e.g., "Currently we are handling 5,500 transactions per minute") then collect them. You can do capacity planning without a workload meter as, in most cases I've worked on, the boss asked for a general scaling of the current load like: "Can we can handle twice our daily peak load?"

It is best to meter when the system is under a stable load, one where the load is not changing rapidly, because then you can get several samples to be sure you are not seeing some odd things that are not connected to the overall load. Below we see some samples where the load is stable over time, but there are things to notice here.

Time	CPU Busy	Disk Busy	TX/Min	Comments
12:00	30%	20%	510	First sample
12:05	31%	21%	523	Load holding stable
12:10	29%	20%	501	Load holding stable
12:15	62%	21%	510	Unusual CPU spike
12:20	31%	22%	537	Back to previous level

Ignoring the sample at 12:15 for the moment, notice that the overall the load is stable. It will never be perfectly stable where each sample gives you exactly the same numbers. Some variation will always happen. Values plus or minus 10% are fine.

If the overall load is never stable, then pick some metered value, like X TX/min, and look at all your samples for any sample you collect that shows X TX/min (± 10%) and see if the other numbers you are tracking, like disk busy and CPU, are stable in relation to it.

In the 12:15 sample the CPU usage essentially doubles even though the disk busy and the TX/min number are stable. This is either some oddball thing that happened and is not normal, or perhaps at 12:15 every day this happens, or perhaps this happens 10 times a day at somewhat random times. Either set yourself to solving this mystery, or if you are sure this is a non-repeating event, ignore the 12:15 data.

This is why you just don't meter for 20 minutes on one day when doing capacity planning. You'll look at lots of data, over many days, and try to come up with a reasonable estimate of how busy everything is under a given load. If there are days where unique demands, not related to load, are placed on your computing world, be sure to meter through those times, too. The whole reason for capacity planning is typically to ensure you have enough resources to handle a peak load, even if it arrives on a day when the system has other things to do, too.

A common mistake people make is to look at the CPU consumption of a process and use that to estimate how much more work it could handle. They might notice that a process is only consuming six seconds of CPU per minute and thus deduce that the process is only 10% busy (60/6 =0.10) but that's usually wrong. Processes do other things besides burn CPU. They wait for disk IO, they wait for other processes to return an answer they need, they wait for resource locks, etc. A process can be doing all the work it can and still burn only a small fraction of the CPU it could if it were just crunching numbers. Gather the per process CPU consumption, but don't mistake it as a straight-forward way to gauge how busy a process is.

When metering for capacity planning, gather any data you can for limits that can be hit. Notice things that kill performance, or sometimes whole applications, when they get full, empty, or reach some magic number. Any limit you hit, will hurt.

Some examples of limits your computing world might hit: disk space, available memory, paging space, licensing limits on the application, number of server processes, maximum queue depth, networking port limits, database limits.

Also consider the limits that per-user or per-directory security and quotas bring to the party. Look for limits everywhere and record how close you are to them.

How To Meter For Load Tests

Load testing is where you give your computing world an artificially generated workload to see how well it holds up. Essentially you can simulate the Christmas rush in July and thus have time to make any needed improvements before the real shoppers show up. Unlike capacity planning, load testing allows you to see response time changes as the load increases.

To create a load test you need to understand what are the major transactions of your current workload and the approximate mix of transaction types. So, for example, at an e-commerce site there might be twenty different types of transactions. However, just four of them make up 85% of the incoming workload and you usually see them in these proportions:

Name	Percent of Total Load
Search For Product	20%
Display Product	50%
Read Comments	5%
Buy	10%
All other transactions	15%

To create a load test you need to understand what your workload looks like. This involves some detective work that is not your normal performance monitoring. You start with a guess about what the most common transaction types are and then look for data that can help you build the table shown above.

Be creative in your search and explore non-traditional sources of information in your company. Extreme precision is not needed here. It matters little if you know that the BUY transaction is 14.67% of the load, as the load is always changing. A nice approximate, well-rounded number will do just fine. Keep in mind that two transactions might be almost identical from a computational perspective. If the X and the Y transactions both access the same files, networks, and processes, then you might decide to lump their percentage of total load together and then use either transaction type for the load test.

Once the load test is designed (you'll find a lot more about that in chapter six) you need to meter the test itself. To do this you look at your computing world with your normal meters that you run every day. During the test, look for two things.

1. Does the load generated by the load test look like the normal load the system sees from real users?

2. How successful was the load test?

You know what the resource utilization looks like for your computing world under a moderate load. Do those numbers look similar to what you see during the load test? If key resources are unusually idle or busy during the load test then the load test itself is not doing the best job of replicating a user-generated load. Again, high precision here is not helpful. If the load test load is close, within 10-20% of the expected user-generated load, that will usually do. However, remember the queuing theory insights from chapter 3. The higher the utilization, the more precise you have to be, because at high utilizations a small increase in utilization can cause a big increase in response time.

Load tests have goals they want to reach that are usually expressed in terms of number of things/sec the system has to handle. Unlike normal user load, a load test generated load starts, stops, and changes at your command. When metering this, you should adjust your metering frequency to capture multiple samples at key parts of the load test and adjust your meter start time so it's nicely synchronized with the load test. In general, you want your meters to start sampling at the top of each minute and be running before, during, and for a while after the load test. The before and after data can help you determine if anything unusual was happening that might have skewed the results.

If the load test achieved its goals, that's great. Report how your computing world handled the load with a focus on any resource that looks like it is close to bottlenecking. Point out queues that are getting long, devices with a high utilization, resources that are close to running out of capacity, etc. Since load tests typically don't simulate all transactions, they tend to under-utilize things. If some resource is close to a limit, you still might recommend adding more just to be safe.

If the load test failed to make its goals, that's unfortunate. Report how your computing world handled the load with a focus on what bottlenecked during the test and what will bottleneck when the test eventually hits its goal load. How does that work? Let's look at the data.

The table below has the results of a load test. The goal was 800 TX/sec. Everything was fine at 200 TX/sec, but the test bottlenecked at 400 TX/sec.

It is clear in the table below that device Y (at 94% busy) will limit any further significant progress towards our goal.

Device name	% Busy at 200 TX/sec	% Busy at 400 TX/Sec
X	25%	50%
Y	47%	**94%**
Z	8%	16%

However, to reach our goal of 800TX/sec, our load test will eventually have to push twice the number of transactions per second through the system. Therefore it is reasonable to assume that every other device in the transaction path will have double the utilization. Take all the utilizations you measured at 400 TX/sec and double them to see what else we would run out of at 800TX/sec.

Device name	% Busy at 200 TX/sec	% Busy at 400 TX/Sec	Projected %busy at the Goal Load of 800 TX/sec
X	25%	50%	**100%**
Y	47%	94%	**188%**
Z	8%	16%	32%

Device X will be at 100% busy at your projected peak. That's never a good thing. Noticing two problems with one load test is smart testing. It will save you time, money and embarrassment. I'd add more X and Y before I tried another load test.

When metering a load test, sometimes there will seem to be a dramatic increase in efficiency where the load test is pushing a lot more transactions through your computing world with dramatically lower resource utilizations. I'm sorry to have to tell you, but this is always bad news.

Computer programs never suddenly get more efficient under a heavy load. What they do is start failing and sometimes it can be faster to fail than to succeed. Returning a simple error message is faster than providing a complex answer. Keep an eye on any reported errors and note any dramatic increase in errors as the load increases.

How To Meter For Building a Model

You build a model to answer a question that capacity planning or load testing can't answer, so all metering efforts for building a model start with the question you are trying to answer. That question has unknown values, some of which metering can fill in.

For example: "How much faster is the storage on the new **UltraBogus 3000**[1] than your current machine?"

You can use load testing to explore the resource consumption and transaction path of a given transaction, by loading the system with that kind of transaction during a relatively quiet time. Any process or resource that shows a dramatic jump in activity is part of the transaction path. Imagine you got this data on a key process before, during, and after a five-minute load test on just transaction X:

	Reads /Sec	Writes /Sec	CPU /Sec
Meters before the load test	2	3	50ms
100 X transactions / sec added with a load test	103	5	654ms
Meters after the load test	4	6	58ms

First notice if the before and after consumption of resources is about the same. If so, it is a good sign that during the load test there was no big change in the user-supplied load. I'd recommend you repeat this test a couple of times. If you get about the same results each time, your confidence will grow, and the possibility of error is reduced.

Now do a bit of simple math to figure out the resource consumption for a given X transaction. For reads it looks as though the number per second increased by about 100/sec during the test, so it's reasonable to estimate that for every X transaction this key process does one read. The writes didn't really change, so no writes are done for the X transaction.

---

[1] The UltraBogus 3000 is a mythical state-of-the art computer of yesteryear whose total downtime has never been exceeded by any competitor. It features fully-puffed marketing literature, a backwards-compatible front door, and a Stooge-enabled, three-idiot architecture that processes transactions with a minimum of efficiency. Its two-bit bus runs conveniently between your office and the repair facility every Tuesday.

For CPU, the consumption during the load test jumped by about 600 milliseconds per second and therefore each X transaction requires 600 / 100 = 6ms of CPU. Overall, this test tells us that the X transaction passes through this key process, does one read, does no writes, and burns six milliseconds of CPU.

Please note, the math will never be precise due to sampling errors and random variations. This methodology can give you a value that is about right. If you need a value that is exactly right, then you need to run this test on an otherwise idle system, perhaps at the end of a scheduled downtime.

You can also use a network sniffer to examine the back and forth network traffic to record the exact nature of the interprocess communication. For political, technical, and often legal reasons, this is a lot easier if you can do this on a test system. Study multiple examples of a given transaction separated in time, or with a ping, so there is no overlap and each unique interaction is clear.

The following timeline was created from the network sniffer data that showed the time, origin, and destination of each packet as these processes talked to each other. During this time there were two instances of the X transaction, a couple seconds apart, and, for clarity, a ping was added so the transaction boundaries were completely clear. We can learn many things from this timeline.

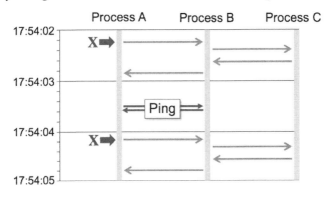

First we know the transaction path for the X transaction (A to B to C to B to A), which can be very useful in building some models. We can also see exactly how long each process works on each thing it receives. Process C worked on each X transaction for about 200 milliseconds before responding. As we learned in chapter 3, if you know the service time you can find the maximum throughput because:

$$\text{MaxThroughput} \leq 1 \,/\, \text{AverageServiceTime}$$

Since this was an idle system, the wait time was zero, so the response time was the service time. If we do the calculation and find that $1/.2 = 5$, then we know that Process C can only handle five X transactions per second.

If the question for the model was: "If we don't reengineer Process C, can we get to 500 X transactions/sec?" The answer is no. If the question for the model was: "How many copies of Process C do we need to handle 500 X transactions a second?" The answer is going to be at least $500/5 = 100$, plus more because you never want to plan for anything to be at, or near, 100% busy at peak.

When it's time to build a model, often you'll need to know things that can be difficult to discover. Share the problem widely as others might have a clue, a meter, or a spark of inspiration that will help you get the data. Work to understand exactly what question the model is trying to solve as that will give you insight as to what alternative data or alternative approach might work.

While you're exploring also keep an eye on the big picture as well. Any model of your computing world has to deal with the odd things that happen once in a while. Note things like backups, end of day/week/month processing, fail-over and disaster recovery plans. Any of these things can affect performance.

Being Ready For a Performance Emergency

Saving the day in a tough situation where performance suddenly and unexpectedly suffers takes two things: the courage to act and preparation.

The courage comes from within, but being prepared is easy; it can happen daily as part of your normal work. Here are some easy things to do.

Have a phone list. When bad things happen, the saddest thing is to watch someone burn valuable time looking up a phone number. When times are good, take the time to make an emergency phone list, and periodically call every number on it to make sure that the number is current, the person still works here, and the person is still responsible for the thing you think they are.

Have a checklist. Make a list of things to do and check in a crisis, as it is easy to forget and overlook things. In the first rush of the problem you might not use it, but when you are stumped, it is a good thing to have.

Know what normal is. On any given day you should have a sense of what is normal in your life. This is also true about your computing world. Before you look at your meters, you should have a good guess as to what they will show you. You develop this skill by first guesstimating what the meter will show and then looking at the results. Do that a couple of times everyday and soon you will know what is normal. This is a wildly valuable skill because the unusual result will jump right out at you, and that is often a big clue as to what's wrong.

Get to know the local experts before you need them. It is likely that your computing world contains so many complex technologies that you can't master them all. Take time in your day to find and build relationships with the other experts in your company. Notice I did not say "meet with." Ignore the bureaucracy, sidestep politics, put away the PowerPoint, talk to them and build relationships. Explore how you can help each other in a time of crisis. I've visited many companies, and the ones that seem to handle problems the best are the ones where the key wizards all know each other.

Master tech support. For some of your computing world the experts are only available through some sort of corporate tech support interface. For any technology you have direct responsibility for, know how to quickly get the help you need. The first time you ever call a vendor's tech support group should not be in a middle of a crisis. Once in a while call tech support with a question. A good first question is: *"I'm preparing for a possible performance problem. Tell me about the diagnostic info would you need from me to get started?"* Find out what meters they want to see and then learn to collect those meters in a fast and efficient way.

Every tech support department has ways to protect their wizards from the simple calls and ways to prioritize problems. If you know the "magic phrase" or options to select, you can get what you need quickly. Learn to work the system. If you are nice, and ask in a casual "oh, by the way..." manner, you can often get them to tell you tricks to adjust the priority or handling of your problem.

Lastly, I've worked with two different computer vendor's tech support people closely and in both cases:

- If you act like a jerk and are mean to the support people, you get the least helpful service from them.

- If you are respectful, calm, prepared, and clear about what you need, then you get their most helpful service.

- If they do something really great for you, take the time to send a short note of thanks to them, with a copy sent to their boss. This will make a big, positive difference in how you get treated next time you call.

Create fast analysis tools. Most of the time your meters are quietly monitoring your computing world at a leisurely pace. When bad things happen, these meters are not designed to answer the question, what's happening NOW. If your regular meters sample the one minute average every five minutes, that won't be very helpful in a crisis. Create easy to start, easy to read analysis tools that can understand what's happening in the last 30 seconds or minute. Every second is valuable in a crisis.

Meter the meters. When you are starting new meters, it is often the case that others will have suspicions that these new meters are somehow hurting the performance. In fairness, I've seen this happen a few times in my career when a hastily edited a metering script was started and immediately went into a tight CPU loop. It is a good thing as part of any metering script to specifically meter the process(s) running the meters. That way, when suspicions arise that your meters are somehow hurting performance, you have the data to defend yourself and your meters.

Never fall in the same hole twice. Every time there is a performance crisis, figure out the root cause and, if possible, add the appropriate meter(s) to your tool set. This advice also applies to situations that were almost at crisis level. A near-crisis is just a real crisis waiting to happen. This time, you caught a break. Next time, you might not be so lucky.

Practice makes perfect. Practice your fire fighting skills by periodically running performance drills. These drills prepare you for action, but they also lead you to ask new questions and find new sources of performance data for your regular monitoring. Ask yourself questions like:

- Response time just got horrible. Can I show that device X is, or is not, the bottleneck?
- Can I show that device X is experiencing errors or
- exhibiting unusual behavior?
- What does normal look like for device X?
- If device X is the problem, who should I call?

Understand the differences in your meters. Many customers I've worked with have a mix of tools to study performance. Some are fancy with beautiful charts and colorful icons, and some are plain simple command line tools. Make sure to understand the differences in how these meters show performance data. These different tools may label things differently, use different low-level meters, sample at a different rate, or average over a different interval.

In a crisis you won't be the only person working on the problem. It is easy for two people looking at two different sets of metering tools to confuse the situation. During the quiet times work to understand those differences and notice what meters always report the same numbers and which ones always differ.

Preserve Your Data

It's just good science and common sense to preserve your collected raw performance data. I can't count the number of times old data suddenly became important. I remember with great embarrassment every instance when I edited the raw data to focus on "the problem" and it turned out that critically important data was deleted. Sigh.

"Always preserve and protect the raw performance data."
– Bob's Fifth Rule of Performance Work

Here are some hints to help keep the data from your performance meters safe and also keep you sane:

- Always work with a copy of your raw performance data, never the original file.

- Make sure your meters don't overwrite previously collected data. If you collect meters as part of a macro or script, take the time to come up with a robust file naming scheme that works for you and will not overwrite previously collected data if the meter has to be restarted unexpectedly. Use that scheme in all your macros/scripts to make it easy to find the right data fast. Remember that in a crisis you might start an additional copy of a macro/script that is tuned slightly differently. Be sure starting a second copy of a script does not wipe out the first one's data, or crash because it can't get write access to the file the first one is already using.

- Never delete old data. Compress (zip) it and leave it for future generations to explore or ignore.

- If you use an external performance monitoring service, periodically download your raw data from their servers and store it locally. Often they will automatically delete data over a certain age.

Performance Monitoring

Chapter 5

CAPACITY PLANNING

"Prediction is difficult, especially about the future."
- Yogi Berra

This chapter shows you how to gain confidence you will make it smoothly though a projected future peak load by scaling up your current observed load.

About Capacity Planning...

A great restaurant is nothing like your computing world. The smells are inviting; alcohol is usually served; success is a direct result of hard physical work; and the workload is primarily moving molecules, not bits. However, just like your computing world, restaurants need capacity planning. Let's explore capacity planning concepts briefly by looking at a 24 hour restaurant.

The restaurant, for most of the day, is calm and relaxed. The load is low and any small problem or delay is easily worked around. However, around mealtimes, the place shifts into high gear, and every thing, every worker and every device, in both the front and the back of the restaurant, has to work  smoothly and efficiently or delays build and customers get cranky. Even if everything is perfect, if more customers show up and demand more service than the place is designed to handle, the wait times will grow and suffering will ensue.

Once the mealtime rush has started, your only option is to endure the consequences of your previous preparations. You and your customers will have to make do with the food you have on hand, the staff who showed up for work, and the devices you have in place to take the orders, cook the food, wash the dishes, etc. If something breaks and there is no spare, you do without. If you run out of a key ingredient, those dishes that depend on it become unavailable, the customers are unhappy, and revenue is lost.

Although each patron is unique, there are big patterns in behavior that the restaurant depends on to function smoothly. At a given restaurant they know that on average 1/3 of the patrons will order a steak and 20% will order dessert. If those ratios change, and suddenly 2/3's of patrons order the steak and everyone orders dessert, that will cause a problem.

Capacity Planning

If the management decides to increase the restaurant capacity to handle double the peak number of customers, then many things have to change. Some of those changes will take months (rebuilding the physical space), some will take weeks (training new staff) and some things (ordering more oysters for the raw bar) can be handled with a phone call. Anything you forget to scale up (dishwashing capacity) can become a bottleneck. If you overbuild for a peak load that never happens, then you are wasting money.

All of the above capacity planning pitfalls and realities apply to your computing world, too. Capacity planning starts with a guess as to how big a future peak load will be. Then you do some research and a little simple math to see if you have enough resources in the right configuration to handle that future load.

What Capacity Planning Can Do For You

Capacity planning is projecting your computing world into a somewhat busier future. If all you are doing is servicing the current workload mix at a faster rate, and the computing environment is staying pretty much the same, then capacity planning is a great tool to use. You can build a capacity plan without understanding the workload mix if you are sure the mix won't change at the peak you are planning for.

Capacity planning gets harder and less useful if the workload mix or the computing/networking infrastructure is changing. If either of these is changing significantly then you should explore the chapter on Modeling.

Capacity planning can fail when a resource, not included in the plan, bottlenecks under the peak load and ruins your post-peak Tiki bar celebration. Capacity planners (i.e. you) should learn from previous failures. If you run out of something, figure out how to meter that thing, and add it to the next capacity plan. Don't fall in the same hole twice.

Capacity plans can succeed brilliantly, yet the users may

suffer because they didn't read the plan and showed up in record numbers that no one expected. As the suffering increases, the mob will grow angry and look for a scapegoat. To be sure it isn't you, it is a good idea to:

- Document the assumptions and goals clearly.

- Get written agreement from the key players.

- Meter the projected peak carefully. If things go badly, hopefully you can show that the load was handled smoothly up to the projected peak and also show under what load the problems started happening.

A well thought out capacity plan can give you hope that you'll sail right though your next peak load with no troubles at all. Once your computing world is tuned-up to handle that load, if you want to turn the hope into confidence, read the chapter on Load Testing.

The Four Numbers of Capacity Planning

In this chapter we'll show how capacity planning for any computing resource is essentially multiplying three numbers together (Utilization * Scaling factor * Safety Margin) and then comparing the result with your maximum utilization for the given resource. If the calculated utilization is greater than the maximum utilization, then you've found a future bottleneck.

The number of times you will repeat this calculation and comparison depends on the size and complexity of your computing environment. Do this for everything that gives you a utilization, like CPUs, disks, etc.

There is a different procedure for handling the things with limits, like free disk space, application limits, etc., later in this chapter.

Utilization

Step one of capacity planning is to find a time that you want to base your capacity plan on. A time when the users are sending your computing world a moderate, stable load and the users are happy with your overall response time and throughput.

Your daily peak load is often a good place to start. Typically that time is decided by watching the system behavior over several days, or weeks, and then selecting some reasonably busy time. Usually, you start by looking at a key system's CPU consumption as it is the one resource that all transactions consume. Let's look at some data and pick a number.

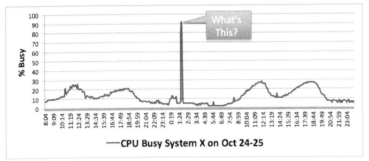

In the above graph you see the CPU busy data from System X sampled every 5 minutes for most of Oct 24th and 25th.

All transactions pass through this computer. The first thing that jumps out at you is the sharp 90%+ busy peak in the middle of the night. A couple of good questions to ask are:

- Is that normal processing or did something go haywire?

- If normal, how often does this happen?

- Does this ever happen during the daily peak user load?

- Are we going to tolerate the response time increases this late-night job creates for about 30 minutes, or do we need to capacity plan for this too?

If this is a background job that runs in the middle of the night when nobody cares about response time, then you can ignore it. If the boss cares about response time 24x7, then you have to plan for this, too.

If this peak is the result of some event that suddenly and rapidly dumps work into the system (e.g. a computer coming back online after a communications disruption) then you need to plan for this. You might still go ahead and build your plan with the normal transaction load, but you'll need to mention the possibility of this spike happening at the worst possible moment in your written capacity plan.

For the moment, let's ignore the early morning peak, and change the scale on the Y-axis so we can see the data we really care about more clearly.

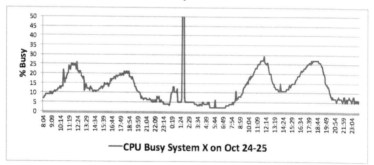

—CPU Busy System X on Oct 24-25

Now that we've trimmed the Y-axis to a max of 50% busy, the next question is which day's peak to use. The daily peaks on the 25th are a bit higher and somewhat more consistent than the daily peaks on the 24th, so let's focus on those peaks and redraw the chart to only show that one day.

Below we can see a sustained 45 minute long peak of 27% busy and a maximum recorded value of 29% busy.

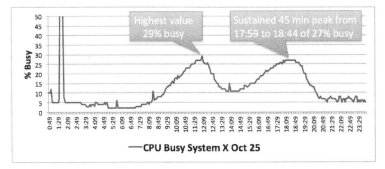

The period where we see the sustained peak, holding steady through multiple samples, is a good place to start. It's good to have multiple adjacent samples in agreement because it gives you confidence that the overall system was at a steady state.

The highest value recorded that day was 29% busy, but you'll notice it is not a sustained peak. Someone may look at that chart and say you have to capacity plan based on the busiest moment. Here it makes little difference as 27% and 29% are not that far apart. However, sometimes there are bigger differences, and sometimes the person insisting on using the highest values is your boss. If your boss is adamant, then go with it. Why fight over a small difference that you can easily correct for in the scaling factor, the safety margin or max utilization values? Pick your battles.

So now you've got two things: a time range for a steady state peak and a value for CPU busy (27%) on this system.

Before you declare victory and go out for a long lunch, look at the metering data from the other systems and devices in your computing world and see if they are showing a peak at about this time with about the same shape. It is entirely possible that the other systems in your computing world did not see this sustained 20 minute peak because it was caused by a little program someone ran unbeknownst to you on this system.

If you want to build a capacity plan based on this observed peak, it should also show up throughout your computing world during the same time and with the same magnitude.

"The meters should make sense to you at all times, not just when it is convenient."
– Bob's Sixth Rule of Performance Work

The Scaling Factor

The scaling factor is a number that represents how much busier the future is anticipated to be when compared with the time you sampled. Sometimes it is based in fact (e.g. you just bought a competitor and you know how much business they will bring), and sometimes it is a guess pulled right out of thin air. To get the scaling factor:

- Collect performance data from your computing world
- Pick a time when the load is moderate and level
- Show your graphs to the key players
- Have them give you the scaling factor

The scaling factor they pick will typically be an SRN (Suspiciously Round Number) and, in my experience, it is never exactly right, but it is often close. Humans are an amazing species. If you are tasked with making this guess, I recommend using the Delphi Technique discussed in chapter three as that can be quite helpful in getting an unbiased group opinion.

Capacity planning assumes that the resource demands of most applications scale linearly because, within normal boundaries, they do. To be precise, 99% of the computer programs I've seen increase their resource consumption in direct proportion to their throughput. If you push twice the work though an application, it will consume close to twice the computing resources such as: CPU cycles, disk IO's, packets sent/received. The exceptions to this rule are:

- When the system or application is starting up. At startup, files have to be opened, programs paged in, caches filled, and initializations performed. Unless you are studying ways to recover faster after a restart/crash, ignore the meters during this time.

- When the application is hopelessly bottlenecked. When overwhelmed algorithms designed to manage about ten things in the queue suddenly have a billion things in queue, they don't work well.

- When errors are happening. They cause retries and retransmissions, poorly tested and inefficient error handling routines to run, processes to crash and restart, and general suffering.

When capacity planning, none of the above apply. You don't capacity plan a system reboot or an application restart, you don't plan to have the peak load experience a bottleneck, and you can't plan for all possible errors. However, you can create a capacity plan or model that takes into account the load being shifted to the remaining systems when a system fails. We'll set aside those unfortunate possibilities until the end of this chapter and the chapter on modeling.

Convert any scaling factor they give you into a multiple of one. So, for example, "Plan for a 30% increase" becomes 1.3, "Twice the load you metered" becomes 2.0.

The Safety Margin

Every company has a level of corporate courage and a

certain aversion to pain. These attributes are shaped by their people, their culture, how much money they have to spend, and by their recent disasters. It is the rare company that likes to hang by a fingernail on the edge of disaster. Only a fool will insist upon planning for a peak load where every resource is at its maximum utilization as there is no margin for error. Most people feel better, and make better decisions, when they have a margin of safety. Besides, capacity planning is not a perfect science:

- The workload mix and intensity are always changing and are somewhat difficult to precisely predict. They are often influenced by such unpredictable forces as the weather, the economy, and your competitors.

- Strange things happen in big companies, and sometimes the demands of other parts of the business on shared resources can change without warning and not in your favor.

- Software upgrades, network changes, equipment swap-outs, and configuration adjustments that happen between the plan and the actual peak can alter performance.

- Capacity planning looks only at the question of "enough." It can give you no hint about the response time changes you will see at the projected peak load. The closer you are to the limit for a given resource, the uglier the response times consequences will be if too much work shows up.

Do not let the person that gave you the scaling factor tell you that it includes the safety margin. You need to keep these two values separate. The scaling factor is your estimate of the future load; the safety margin is how sure you are about that estimate.

The safety margin inflates your projected utilizations by the percentage that you choose. Most companies I've worked with have chosen a safety margin value between 10% and 50%, with the most common values in the 20% range. When using this in capacity planning, convert it into a multiple of one. A 20% safety margin becomes 1.2.

Max Utilization

For resources that provide a service there is a utilization beyond which the delays caused by queuing effects become too painful. As a general rule: the slower the resource is, the lower this pain threshold should be. Why? It's all about wait time and service time.

The busier the resource is the more likely you'll have to wait in a queue to be serviced and the longer that queue will be. Each thing ahead of you in the queue will have its full measure of service time before you get to run.

How Busy Is Too Busy?

As we learned in chapter 3, any device that is 50% busy will have an average response time of twice the service time as there is an average of one job to be processed before you get your turn to use the device. The slower the device is, relative to the other things in your computing world, the more painful this math becomes. Think about it this way... Which would you rather see doubled: the cost of your next haircut or the cost of your next mortgage payment?

In the early 21st century computers used spinning magnetic disks for long-term storage. Disks were the slowest part of any computer system by several orders of magnitude and thus, the rule of thumb was to keep the utilization of a disk below 50%. If we switch to solid state disks, their vastly lower service time, which translates into a lower wait time and thus a lower response time for a similarly busy device, would justify picking a higher max utilization number.

When picking the max utilization for a device, there is always the temptation to shove money into the discussion with comments like: Those disks were very expensive, and now you are telling me I can only use X% of their capacity. Your reply to incredulous comments like that should point out, in a gentle way, that the cost of running some device at 100% busy is remarkably bad response times for the customers – see queuing theory.

Device exclusivity plays a big part in the number you pick for max utilization as well. When a process needs CPU, any one of the multiple CPU's in the system will do. If you can go to many places to get serviced then the odds are good that one of them will be free and that will hold down response time as the utilization climbs toward 100%.

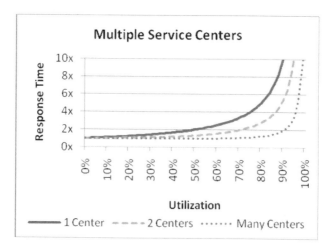

On the other hand, if the data you need is on one device (e.g. reading a specific record from disk), then you can only go to that device, and the response time curve turns ugly at a much lower average utilization.

To pick a max utilization number for a given device, start by doing your homework; read the manuals, search the web, and then talk to the vendor. If you are laughing at my suggestion to start by reading rather than calling, remember that when you call, you will end up talking to either: people who don't know, so they bluff and bluster, or people who do know. If you start as an informed person, you can quickly identify and disregard the people who don't know. If you luck out and get to talk to someone who does know, they are more likely to give you a rich and complete answer because it is clear that you've done your homework.

When calling, I've had the best luck starting with the technical sales people who are assigned to your account, and then people in the professional services or customer service group. Also remember that questions of max utilization have direct impact on how many of these devices your company will buy. People may be very cautious in their responses because nobody working for a vendor wants to screw up a potential sale.

You can also experimentally select a max utilization value of some resource through testing by adding load to the resource until you see the response time start to grow unacceptably. The number you get should be between 50% (for really slow resources) and 80-90% for the speediest resources where the incoming work also has many service centers to choose from.

It is not that hard to write a program that keeps some device busy, but busy is not the same thing as backed-up with work. The real response time pain of a busy device comes from the line of transactions waiting to run before you do.

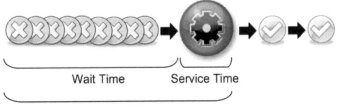

If your busy program is just one process that submits a transaction and then waits for it to complete, you won't create a long line of waiting transactions. Your response time will equal your service time and you won't feel the pain of a long queue of waiting transactions.

How Busy Is Too Busy For A Process

A process executes code until it has to wait for something like a reply from another process, a lock, or an IO to complete. CPU consumption for a process does not tell the whole story of how busy it is. Here are some guidelines to help you figure that out:

- With rare exception, a process that is 100% CPU busy (burns one second of CPU per second) can't do anything more for you, has most likely hit a bug, and is doing nothing useful for you.

- A common performance analysis mistake is to assume that a process consuming only a small amount of CPU couldn't possibly be the bottleneck. Processes wait for things, and when they wait, they consume no CPU.

- If the software has remained unchanged since the last peak load, you can take the per process CPU utilization data from that peak and feel pretty sure that process can consume at least that much CPU at the next peak.

- Some applications have a dynamically tunable number of processes doing a given task. Often they have the same name (e.g. FE01, FE02, FE03...) with a number appended to it. If the load is spread evenly, you only need to study one example of each group. You can create an artificial peak load for those processes by reducing their number and letting the incoming workload overwhelm them for a minute, or two, while you gather some metering data. Then start additional processes to return things to normal. Note: This is not a perfect test, but it is better than nothing.

- If you can see the queue of incoming requests for a given process and that queue is never empty, it's clear that the process is working about as fast as it can, regardless of how little CPU it consumes. However, that process may not be the root cause of the bottleneck. In the example below, for every transaction Process X works on, it has to ask the somewhat slower Process Y for a reply before proceeding. Process Y is on a different machine, and that is why you can see Process X bottleneck and backup even though there are plenty of resources on System X.

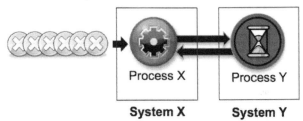

System X   **System Y**

- Use your common sense. If you are planning for a peak that is ten times the load you are currently measuring, and the process in question is already consuming 0.2 seconds of CPU/second, then clearly this process will be using 10 * 0.2 = 2 seconds of CPU/second, which is impossible.

- Some processes are involved in the main transaction path, and some come into play less often. Focus your efforts on the main transaction path processes. How do you identify them? The processes that consume most of the resources and whose consumption rises and falls as the load does are the processes you want to study. They are typically a small subset of all the processes running.

- If none of the above suggestions work for you, then you either have do some load testing or make a good faith estimate. When estimating, include others in the process and use the Delphi Technique as described in chapter 3.

When you have a max utilization (expressed as a number from zero to one) for all your resources then you are ready to do some capacity planning.

Doing The Math of Capacity Planning

Now you are ready to scale up to the projected peak load. The formula is straight forward:

Utilization * Scaling Factor * Safety Margin = Projected Peak

Imagine you have a resource that is 40% busy (utilization is 0.4), and you need to plan for a peak load that is 50% larger than what you are seeing now (scaling factor is 1.5), and you are reasonably sure of your projected peak load within about 10% (safety margin is 1.1).

Doing the math you get 0.4 * 1.5 * 1.1 = 0.66 and now you know this resource will be 66% busy at the projected peak load. You've determined the max utilization for this resource is 75%, and so you feel reasonably sure that this resource will not be a bottleneck at your projected peak. Now do that calculation for all your other resources.

When presenting capacity planning results, you can quickly overwhelm the audience with numbers and, despite their keen interest in your results, they will stop listening, reading, and caring after just a few sets of this data. To help them absorb the results, show the data graphically and use the same colors, line size, and wording in each chart for the measured, projected, and maximum utilizations. That way a quick glance is all that is needed to know if there is a problem at the projected peak and how close to the max utilization this thing is. Also take into consideration that you'll be projecting your results in color, but your audience likely will be holding a greyscale photocopy in their hand. Strive for clarity.

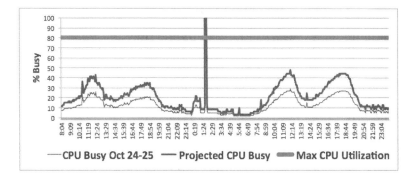

Capacity Planning For Limits

There are many things that can kill performance that are measured in terms of "full" rather than "busy" such as disk storage space. Also, many things have arbitrary limits (max = 10) that, when hit, can bring on great suffering. To capacity plan for these things, you need to look for limits. Typically, you'll find those limits buried in the documentation. Read the manuals, especially the programming manuals. Clues to limits often show up in the arguments to subroutine calls. Yes, this is tedious. I did it. You can do it too.

Disk Storage

Disk is a form of storage that is persistent. Reboot and the data previously stored there is still there.

- Storage requirements are sensitive to the total number of transactions processed, not the peak transaction rate.

- Over time, storage tends to fill, but there are endless variations as to how that happens, as temp files are deleted, end-of-month processing happens, and old data is migrated. To plan for this you need to watch the resource over a longer period of time to see the trends in demand.

- You may have to plan for a different time scale than your next projected peak because the remedy for a full storage problem might be something that can only be done during scheduled maintenance periods, or when money is available next year.

- Way too much of a resource can be a problem, too. Not a performance problem, but a political one. Budgets are tight and "wasted" resources are targets.

Memory

You can run out of memory, but memory is different from other types of storage. Anything that doesn't fit in memory, and is not immediately needed, can be stored on disk.

- Memory demands tend to be rather constant in the face of increasing loads. The first few transactions will page everything into memory and fill the disk cache buffers.

- You don't run out of memory, like you run out of milk. If a page of memory is needed for something new, the data in an old page is sent out to disk, like storing your old college chemistry book in the attic. This is an efficient thing to do if you are not going to need that page for a while.

- The CPU fetches the code and the data from memory to do the work. If the CPU has to wait for code or data pages to be fetched from disk, that is very bad for performance. If that is happening on a regular basis, fix it.

- If there is a memory leak, processes running that leaky code will tend to get bigger over time. When searching these out, remember that the leaked memory is often paged out, as it is not active. Be sure to check the meters looking at total memory allocated, not total active memory.

- Leaky and long lived processes can leak enough memory to run out of address space, causing them to crash, or exhaust the system's paging space, which usually brings down the whole system. No fun there.

- Typically, you can't add more memory unless you reboot the system. In this 24x7 world, that can be problematic. However, most operating systems will allow you to adjust the amount of memory the disk cache uses. Try that first.

- Memory upgrades tend to come in big multi-gigabyte increments. If your meters are showing you need more memory, you don't have to calculate exactly how much more you need since your next step up will bring a huge increase in memory.

File System

Data is typically stored in some sort of file structure. These structures have limits as to how large files can be, how much data can be stored in a given record, if files can span disks, etc. It will take some digging, but you can bring these limits to light and find out if you are close to any of them.

- The more modern the operating system you are working on the more ridiculously large these limits are, but it is the rare shop that doesn't have some old code running on old technology. Start with those machines.

- Files typically have some form of locking to prevent multiple processes from messing up the file. It is often the case you can grow a file big enough to handle a peak, but often the right thing to do is to split the file so that locking is not a performance limit.

- Files live in directories and those can have max size limits that can stop things dead in their tracks.

- It is best not to use directory size limits to control file growth on production systems.

OS and Application Limits

There are many programs and operating systems have that have hard limits on the maximum number of things.

- These limits might be a licensing decision based on money or an engineering limit based on the size of some key data structure designed eight releases ago. In any case, don't just assume if you have 10 of something the software will let you have 15.

- If your capacity plan requires you to scale things up, test that scaling long before the peak to make sure some other limit doesn't bite you.

- Like it or not, there are application and operating system limits that you don't know about. Be curious, and look for them in your spare time. Sadly, sometimes you find them by slamming into them. Once you pay that price, meter that limit and build it into your next capacity plan.

Monsters Under The Bed

You cannot prove a negative. For example, you can't prove there are no monsters waiting to get you while you sleep because no matter how carefully you check, you might overlook some spot (like the closet) where they are hiding.

What you've learned about bottlenecks and Liebig's Law in chapter three clearly shows that even a small and obscure part of the transaction path can become a major bottleneck if given enough work to do.

Capacity planning should not be sold as a guarantee that all will be well at the next peak. No matter how good a performance person you are, you can't offer that guarantee. Capacity planning is more like a pre-trip checklist to ensure you have what you need, and all systems on this list are good-to-go. Invariably, you will go on that trip, and somewhere along the way you'll discover you forgot X, don't have enough Y, and for the first time ever you need Z. That's all bad news, but remember that your capacity planning effort found bottlenecks that would have limited your throughput even more.

So, do capacity planning to the best of your ability with the things you do know about. Then, if you get caught short on some resource, take the time before the next big peak to learn about that resource and to do a more complete plan next time. Unless this is the last peak before you retire, you need to think long-term.

It's Not JUST About The Peak

Even though capacity planners naturally tend to focus on the peak minute of the peak hour of the peak day, remember that most complex commercial systems have other stresses in their lives. These are the additional things to factor in when picking a good time to start capacity planning:

- Off-peak downtimes where some fraction of the hardware is offline and the total load is carried by what remains
- Backups
- Nightly reports and other batch jobs

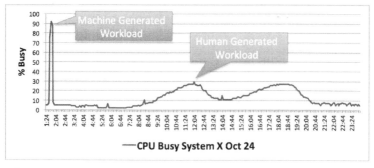

—CPU Busy System X Oct 24

Above you see the classic performance signature of machine driven work, a nearly instant-on load with no normal change in intensity as the day progresses. Also, the work runs through the system at a relentless pace because there is no think time.

Sometimes a well thought out solution that works during a peak day kills you at night, kills you on the weekend, or kills you at the end of the month or quarter. Don't just meter the peaks. Meter all year, and notice when these timed or special events happen. Pay particular attention to:

• Which files get busy

• Where the communications traffic is flowing

• Scheduled maintenance periods

When To Do Capacity Planning

Every organization is different. Some are nimble, some ponderous and slow, some have money to burn, and some won't see new hardware for years. You need to factor these realities into your plans as capacity planning is only helpful when it is done with enough lead time to fix the discovered future bottlenecks. Some things to consider:

• There are times when money is available in your budget and usually a time by which you have to spend it or lose it. Any purchases you plan for have to hit this window.

- How long does it typically take your company to complete a major purchase once the decision has been made to buy? A new computer that arrives two weeks after the seasonal peak doesn't do you any good.

- How fast can your vendor build, deliver and install the thing you need? Some things you can have tomorrow; some things take months to build and deliver.

- Do you want to wait for the newest/fastest machine just on the horizon or go with last year's model now?

- Are there any company-wide spending edicts in place?

- When is the end of the quarter for key vendors? Buying hardware at the end of the quarter (especially the fourth quarter) puts you in a better bargaining position.

With time all things are possible, so the best advice is to start as soon as you can.

Capacity Planning For Tough Times

There are two situations where you create capacity plans that assume you have less computing resources than you have now: disaster recovery and budget cutting. In both cases the first thing that needs to be done is make some hard business decisions about suffering and money.

Suffering

Is your company willing to let the users feel a little response time pain if a key system or device fails in order to save some money? Every company I've ever worked for had a different answer, and that answer changed depending on the market they live in, and their current financial situation.

As a capacity planner, you are looking for a clear statement about response time and throughput goals such as:

- If _____ fails, our customers shouldn't feel a thing even if it happens on the busiest day of the year.

- If _____ fails, our customers shouldn't feel a thing on an average day. We are willing to gamble that this will not happen on the busiest day of the year.

In the above bullets _____ is the thing you are considering doing without and could be as small as a comm line or as large as a whole datacenter.

Money
At the end of the day, it is all about money. If you are asked to capacity plan for less hardware, and the chief consideration is money, then you need some numbers to work with:

- How much money is the company trying to save?

- Where are they looking for savings: hardware cost, software licensing, facilities, etc.?

- In round numbers, what are the savings per unit of hardware, software, floor space, etc.?

In many ways this is like playing the game Monopoly™ when you are low on cash. Suddenly you need to pay rent, so you have to return your buildings to the bank for the cash you need. You will select those buildings based on what they are worth and what they could make in rent as the game goes forward. The same is true in capacity planning. If the boss says he needs to save $200,000 in costs, then you need to know what eliminating a given machine will save you.

Dealing With Disaster

When planning for disaster, decide what part(s) of your world will be suddenly unavailable, and then mathematically shift the load to the still-working parts of your world.

For example, your overall projected peak load is 150 transactions per second (TPS), and you have three front end machines that each take 1/3 of that load. To capacity plan for handling that peak load with one of the front end machines down, just divide the peak load by two machines rather than three. So at peak the two remaining machines will each need to handle 150TPS / 2 = 75TPS.

On a normal, non-peak day, each front end machine handles about 25TPS during the busiest part of the day, and the measured utilization of system resources is what you are going to use to scale up the load. To get the scaling factor you need for your capacity plan, divide your per-machine projected peak load by the measured load.

If at peak everything is working normally, each front end machine will be handling 150TPS / 3 = 50TPS, and thus it will be doing twice the work 50TPS / 25TPS = 2X of your metered day.

If at peak one front end machine emits a puff of greasy black smoke and dies, then the remaining two machines will each be handling 150TPS / 2 = 75TPS, and thus they will each be doing three times the work 75TPS / 25TPS = 3X of your metered day.

When doing this work, you can also scale the disaster up to the datacenter level (What if a hurricane takes out our North

Carolina datacenter?) or down to a single communications line. You just have to figure out if X breaks, what fraction of the pre-failure load will the remaining hardware have to pick up. Then add that to the projected peak for which you are capacity planning and do the math.

There are as many disaster scenarios as there are things that can break. You might get overwhelmed thinking of all the possible combinations, but remember, you don't have to plan for all scenarios, just the worst ones. If you need to plan for various troubles that will leave System X carrying 110%, or 250%, or 300% of the metered load, do the math for the worst case first. If the system can handle a 300% load increase, it can clearly handle 250% or 110% easily.

Budget Cuts

When looking to reduce equipment costs, you have to figure out how to do more, with less. It is almost never the case that there is some easily applied magic fix. Instead, typically, workload has to be moved to fewer systems which entails some unforeseen consequences and some risk to the stability and availability of your computing world. It can be done, but there are some things to which you need to pay attention:

- Computers are not interchangeable homes for processes as they have different hardware that can support different versions of operating systems. Clearly applications designed for the X operating system won't run on the Y operating system. That's obvious. What is often missed, is there can be compatibility problems between version 10.1 and 10.2 of operating system X. Sometimes the hardware you plan to keep can only run 10.2, but the third-party code you depend on has a nasty bug in their 10.2 release and so you need to hold at 10.1.

- Computers need to connect to the world, and some of them may require specific hardware that is only available on specific machines and versions of operating systems.

- There are always the issues posed by who "owns" each machine and how that that machine is accounted for in the budget. Even if you save the company $50,000, if that money is not in the right part of the budget, it doesn't solve your problem.

- There may be legal limits preventing you from having unencrypted data on certain networks or security constraints that prevent certain people with admin-level privileges from access to certain systems.

- Whatever plan you come up with can't screw up your disaster recovery plans.

- If you're planning to turn off some piece of hardware, then you need to account for everything going through that machine. Frequently, there is more interconnectivity and dependency than you see at first.

- Processes have all sorts of connections, communication paths, and shared resources. Some of these run much slower when accessed across the net vs. locally. Some can only work if the processes are on the same machine.

- Whatever files or databases you move will need storage space and a sensible way to back them up.

- Speaking of files, it is amazing how many files a process needs, with some of them only accessed on special occasions. When you change the file structure it is not at all unusual to find critical files that have been completely forgotten by the local experts. Also, changes to directory and file access permissions (read, write, execute) can cause trouble. Plan to spend considerable time hunting files, finding connections, and debugging the results of the move.

- When moving a process between machines with different CPU speeds, if the two machines are made by the same vendor, they can usually give you a reasonable number to scale the CPU utilization. If moving to a different vendor's machine, you might just have to do your own testing.

Doing the work of moving workload, processes, files, and networks is a deeply detail-oriented, complex task. Start by creating your plan with what you know, then spend time checking all the things on this list and whatever else you think of. Most of your plan will work, some of it won't. Adjust and recheck all your assumptions. Repeat this plan/recheck process until it all seems to work while keeping your boss in the loop to be sure the money saved is sufficient and the politics are working out as well. If significant reengineering is required to make this work, also read the Modeling chapter.

The Human Response

When you present your capacity plan be prepared for at least one round of adjustments. Even with the safety margin and max utilization values built into the calculations, some managers will still be uncomfortable with your results.

Sometimes you are too close to a limit, and the boss will have you add resources to the plan. Sometimes a resource is seen as "too idle", and that will bother them. Sometimes your results do not support their empire building goals or cost savings targets, and you'll be asked to change the plan.

Adjustments can be made, but do what you can to make sure the plan sticks to the truth. If your boss tries to force you to lie or profoundly fudge the numbers or "reframe the truth", do your best to resist.

Capacity Planning Limits

Capacity planning has its limits. It can't predict the response time you'll experience under the future load. Also, as you make adjustments to your computing world (move this load here, upgrade that computer, plan for more transaction X and less transaction Y) capacity planning becomes less and less accurate and more uncertain.

At some point, as the complexity builds, you have to do load testing to physically test your computing world, or you have to go beyond capacity planning into modeling. Each approach has its drawbacks and benefits which you will find in the chapters ahead. For now, here are some general guidelines to help you choose:

- Modeling is better for evaluating the relative wonderfulness of potential design strategies, as no expensive and time consuming coding/rewiring is required to run the model.

- Load Testing can only be done on things that exist.

- Modeling and load testing can predict future response times under load, but most managers I've worked with feel much more confident in believing load test results.

- Modeling is often an easier way to thin out the bad ideas by quickly showing that proposals 1 and 3 will not work.

- Load testing is the best way to show that things that require third party content will work with reasonable response time under a given load, as you can't model the third party.

Chapter 6

LOAD TESTING

"In theory there is no difference between theory and
practice. In practice there is."
                                          - Yogi Berra

This chapter gives you practical advice on how to load test
an existing application to see if can really handle the
upcoming peak.

About Load Testing...

With good performance monitoring you can see what is
currently causing a problem and gather important
performance data. With good capacity planning you can
project the measurements of the current workload into a
busier future and see where trouble may lie.

All that is good and useful, but there is nothing quite as
reassuring as watching your computing world smoothly

handle a workload of synthetically generated transactions long before the real peak arrives.

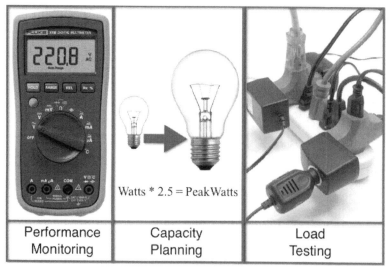

| Performance Monitoring | Capacity Planning | Load Testing |

Watts * 2.5 = Peak Watts

The fundamental reason you go through all the trouble of a load test is to buy yourself time to fix things and to save money. You could just wait for the peak you are planning for to come naturally and hope for the best. If it works, then all is well. If not, then you have no time to fix anything, no time to test the fixes, and only the most expensive options to fix things remaining on the table. The company will have to throw money and hardware at the problem and endure significant risk with untested workarounds. If performance is bad, there will be additional costs as customers move to your competitors, and the call center spends a lot more time saying "we're really sorry" to the customers who bother to call.

Load testing can also increase your confidence in your capacity planning efforts and show where you have way too much of a given resource, both of which can save your company serious money as you may be able to narrow the safety margin.

Creating The Load

In real life, the users of your computing world generate the workload. In load testing, you define the workload. You need to know the individual transactions (e.g., deposit, withdraw) that make up the workload, the right ratio of these transactions (e.g. ten withdraw transactions for every deposit transaction), and figure out at what rate you want them delivered to emulate the peak load.

All of this will take some creative application performance metering and some discussions about which transactions to emulate. Let's tackle these problems one at a time, but first a word about abandoning your quest for perfection.

Good Enough Is Just Fine

Give up on the idea of perfection. There is no "perfect" in load testing, as the users are always changing their behavior and you will never emulate all the different transactions with all the possible user choices. Why?

Unlike capacity planning, where you can do your work by yourself with a spreadsheet and some metering data, load testing costs money, often requires the help of others, and can be disruptive. Also, load testing is usually done at an hour that is inconvenient for everyone involved. All of this tends to push back hard against perfection.

You are looking for "good enough" to get the job done. There are many choices you'll have to make and guesses you'll have to take, so how do you know the load test you've designed is good enough?

Test Validation

When you've designed and built your load test, run it at a normal everyday load and see if it works without errors and returns performance meter values that are similar to the ones you get on an average day. This is known as test validation.

For example, at noon on a pre-peak day your computing world is handling 50 TX/sec, and a key machine is around 20% busy. At midnight that machine is almost idle. You are planning for an upcoming peak that is four times (4X) the noon peak. If your load test reasonably emulates the real user load, then when you run your load test at midnight, sending in 50 TX/sec, the key machine should show 20% busy, and the other key meters in your computing world should also resemble their noon time values. If half your computing world is idle under this test, clearly you've got more work to do. If the numbers are close enough, then your test is good to go. But, what's close enough?

Begin with the peak in mind. The peak you are planning for is 4X the normal noon load of 20% busy. Any differences in the meters between the real user load and the midnight load test will be 4x greater at the peak, and that means little unimportant differences can become big significant differences. Let's look at the numbers on three key meters in the table below.

	Real User Load Measured At Noon	Midnight Load Test
Meter X	20%	19%
Meter Y	30%	20%
Meter Z	10%	8%

Meter X matches up nicely. If we were emulating the real user load perfectly we'd expect meter Y and meter Z to match up nicely as well, but they don't.

Meter Y is much busier at noon than during the midnight load test. Here it makes a difference, as we expect the peak to be 4X the measured day. So just using basic capacity planning two things are clear:

1. The resource watched over by Meter Y will bottleneck at peak as: 30% * 4 = 120%

2. This is a difference that makes a difference, as Meter Y during the load test only showed a utilization of 20% busy and that works out to 20% * 4 = 80% at peak. Meter Y tells us we have more work to do on this load test.

Meter Z is a little off between the noon and the midnight numbers, but this is a difference that you could live with because, even when you scale up the larger sample (10% * 4 = 40%), it's clear this is not going to be a bottleneck.

You can also do this checking with any meter that counts things of importance to you like packets, IO's, thingamajigs, whatever. Once the results are close enough, you can trust that your load test will do a good job pushing your computing world as hard as the users will at peak. Now, let's design a load test.

Selecting Transactions To Emulate

Your computing world handles many different types of transactions, but the bulk of the workload, and/or the bulk of the revenue, comes from just a few of them. It is also the case that many transactions have important differences for users but are computationally identical for your computing world – the bits flow through the same processes and consume the same resources.

Start building a list of transactions to emulate. First add the ones that make up the bulk of your workload. Then add any transactions that bring serious money into the company even if they are not all that numerous.

"To a corporation, nothing is more important than money. Follow the money."
– Bob's Seventh Rule of Performance Work

Then add any transactions that have recently caused you trouble and are thus politically sensitive at this time. Now look that list over and, if it makes things simpler, you can combine transactions that are computationally similar into a generic transaction – the buyX, buyY and buyZ transactions get grouped together into the generic buyStuff transaction. This will typically leave you with a short list of transactions.

Scripting Transactions

Users are not identical robots typing the same things over and over at machine-like speeds.

Users are unique, they pause to consider and to choose, and they do different things. There are constraints (logical, legal, and practical) as to what your users can do. You can't login simultaneously from two different cities, you can't withdraw with a zero balance, and you can't put a trillion things in your shopping cart. Whatever generates the load for your load test has to be able to handle that. Specifically look for load generation tools that have a way to:

- Record a script of actions to follow for each type of transaction you decide to emulate

- React to varying information presented during the transaction, such as security questions

- Determine if the response indicates success or failure ("Deposit accepted" vs. "D603 Database error...")

- Add variability to that script by doing different things on each visit

- Authenticate themselves so your security software will allow these transactions through

- Build think time between steps of a transaction to emulate the behavior of real users as they pause and consider

Scripting transactions takes work. First you get it to work once, then you add variability into it (different users doing different things), and then you find security or reasonableness checks you have to either deal with or work around. For multi-step transactions (e.g., login, shop, buy), you need to test at each step to see if it was successful and to "report & abort" the transaction if it was not.

Typically, you work on one transaction at a time, testing it over and over until you are satisfied. Then you create and test the next transaction. When you've got all the transactions in your load test working and tested individually, then you test them together, typically at low-power, to convince yourself that they all work together smoothly. Look for the results you see in the meters to match up nicely with the meters you get from the normal load generated by real users.

Generating The Load
Something has to generate the load for your load test. Depending on your situation you might build it yourself, buy it, or have some company generate the load for you, typically through the Internet. Here are some things to look for when evaluating your options.

Location
Where you generate the load matters. The load should flow though as much of your computing world as it would normally. Any part of your computing world that you do not test is, by definition, untested. That untested part is likely to keep you up at night worrying and surprise you, in

an unpleasant way, during the peak with its shocking lack of throughput.

If you are doing a stand-alone load test of a small subsystem, then the generated load should come from outside the tested computer(s). Why? First, it takes resources to generate load, and you'd like a clean set of performance data from the tested system(s). Also, if you generate the load on the tested system, then you are not testing the network connections though which the real load will have to flow.

If you are doing an end-user load test, then the load should be generated outside your company and from the locations where your users live. As you saw in chapter four, distance matters on the Internet.

Ease Of Use

The sales pitch for the load test tool will tend to focus on the beauty and the flexibility of how it displays results. That's all good, but you'll spend a lot more time creating and debugging the load test than you will spend running and evaluating it. When selecting a load generation tool carefully note:

- The ease with which you can create new transactions and modify existing ones.

- The quality and clarity of diagnostic info you get back when transactions are failing.

- How easily and rapidly the tool can schedule, stop, and restart tests. Load testing is a team sport. Making people wait for you, and the load testing tool, is never fun.

- How close to real time do you get the results for transactions started and competed, transaction response time and failure rate. You want the bad news as soon as possible, so you can stop, fix, and restart the test.

Money

Generating load costs money. More load, more money. Budget for the testing you'll have to do before the big load test, and plan to work though a couple of failures where you have to stop the test, fix something, and restart it.

Types Of Load Tests

The way you tune the settings of your load test is determined by what questions you need answered. It is not just about the next big peak. There are several different kinds of load tests: Test Validation, Load Testing, Isolation Testing, Stress Testing, and Endurance Testing.

Test Validation

As described earlier in this chapter, this is a load test where you are testing the load test itself to see if it emulates a moderate real user load with "good enough" fidelity. The key output of this test is confidence in the test, not the charts and graphs it creates.

Once you and the other key stakeholders believe that this test will scale up to create a believable user load, then you can move on to the actual load testing.

Load Testing

A load test applies a realistic external load that simulates the anticipated peak to directly measure response time, throughput, and other key internal performance meters. A load test can show you under what load the response time and throughput will start to get ugly. It also can:

- Validate your capacity planning efforts or show you where an unrecognized bottleneck exists

- Allow you to calibrate your meters, and other performance information gathering tools, under a very stable load

- For example:
  - At 500 TX/sec the bamboozle/sec meter = 2000
  - At 1000 TX/sec the bamboozle/sec meter = 4000
  - So each TX (on average) generates four bamboozles

Now you can use the bamboozle/sec meter any time as a workload meter by dividing it by four, even though you have no clue what a "bamboozle" is.

Isolation Testing

In a load test you control the mix of transactions, so you can feed your computing world a pure stream of only one kind of transaction, rather than the mix of transactions the users usually generate. This can be a useful way to explore your computing world.

You can see the resources consumed by each type of transaction tested, which can be very useful in model building. Notice if there are any systems or resources that you did not expect this type of transaction to use? If a performance meter surprises you, you have more work to do.

If you are hunting a problem, or checking to see if some change to your computing world made a difference in performance, isolation testing can help. By testing the major transaction types separately, you might find that only the X transaction has dramatically slowed down or that only the Z transaction causes the problems you are seeing.

An isolated test of a transaction made of distinct parts (e.g., a web-based transaction that visits the home page, searches, and then puts that thing in a cart) can show you clearly which part of the longer transaction is having performance troubles under what load.

Web Transactions	Home Page Time	Search Time	Cart Time
100/sec	1.2 sec	0.8 sec	0.5 sec
200/sec	1.2 sec	2.1 sec	0.6 sec
300/sec	1.3 sec	8.3 sec	0.7 sec

Since you ran this transaction in isolation, the metering data you are getting from your computing world is only showing work generated by this kind of transaction. That makes it easier to find the bottleneck. Clearly from the table above the Search part of this transaction is having some problems at 200 TX/sec and is really hurting at 300 TX/sec. The performance meters during this load test should give you a big clue as to where the problem lies.

Stress Testing

A stress test is just a load test where you purposely overdrive the system to find its breaking point. This is done by running a load test with a normal transaction mix, but with way too many users and/or no think time.

If you run your load test and you achieve your goals it is still useful and interesting to push the system to its breaking point to see exactly how it breaks – so you know it when you see it. Would you want to go to a doctor who had studied medicine carefully, but never seen a really sick person?

Endurance Testing

This is a load test where you study if everything in your computing world can keep running over time, not just for a few minutes. Typically, the load is well below the peak load, and what you are looking for are things that you can run out of or that don't scale well. Common questions to look at are:

- How much disk capacity is consumed per transaction?

- How much memory is leaking per transaction?

- Is there an unknown hard coded limit in the software?

- Is throughput and response time just as good after the millionth transaction (when files are bigger, databases age, and sorting algorithms are challenged) as it was for the early transactions?

These tests are important to run before software is put into production as stopping and fixing problems in the middle of the day on the live system is usually not an option the company wants to take.

When To Load Test

When driving, it is best to start applying the brakes when you have enough time to easily avoid disaster. In load testing, it is best to start your efforts when you have enough lead-time to fix any performance problem you uncover. That amount of time is different for every situation as there are many things that will influence your decision as to when to get started.

All organizations have a pace at which they feel comfortable. This is especially true when spending money. A good first question to ask yourself when it looks likely that you'll have to spend to get though the next peak is "How long did it usually take between decision and delivery of the last few major IT purchases?" Every company is different, and I've personally seen behavior ranging from 30 days to almost two years. You need to do your work with enough lead-time to take this into account. Don't get me wrong, change can happen faster than this, but it is just a lot more pleasant for everyone involved if you take into account the company's normal pace.

There are many other factors that influence when to test. Weigh each one as you choose the best time to do your work.

- The annual pre-peak hardware/software freeze

- The anticipated dates for big infrastructure changes

- The anticipated dates for the roll out of new websites, applications, or features

- The last quarter of the fiscal year for key vendors

- When money is available in your budget

As you will see in the list above, when taking all factors into account, there might not be an ideal time to do the load test. In that case, pick your battles and begin your work. With time, all things are possible. In general, earlier is better.

Load Test Goals

A load test either achieves a certain goal, or it dies trying. If your computing world crumbles half way to that goal, then your performance meters should contain some good clues as to what to fix, improve, reengineer, or upgrade before you try again. However, you need goals to shoot for, and you need them early in the whole load test process.

The goals for the load test are based primarily on what your computing world has handled during past peaks, plus an increase for the projected growth between peaks.

All load test goals boil down to just a few questions. How hard are you going to push your computing world? What response time is acceptable? What error rate is acceptable? What internal meters will you collect?

How Hard To Push

If what you are testing is user visible, then you may frame your goals for how many virtual users will be simultaneously supported. In real life, each user will submit work at a given pace and, for multi-step transactions, usually wait between steps as they read and think about the results of the previous step. This leads to two different ways of counting virtual users: concurrent and simultaneous.

Concurrent virtual users are connected to the system and are requesting work at some regular interval. **Simultaneous virtual users** are all requesting work at the same time.

If your computing world was a bar, then the concurrent virtual users would be all the patrons in the bar, and the simultaneous virtual users would be the patrons who are currently asking the bartender for a drink.

If you were running a load test as a stress test where the wait time was zero, then concurrent virtual users equal simultaneous virtual users as every patron would be guzzling each drink served and immediately requesting a new one.

If your boss wants the goal stated in terms of the number of simultaneous transactions, or users, then all you need to do is set the think time to zero and use enough virtual users to match the goal number, plus a few extra. What are the extra for? Once a virtual user finishes a transaction, it takes some non-zero time to report the results and reset itself to go again. You can figure out the right number of extra virtual users when you are doing the low-power test validation testing. The shorter the transaction is in relationship to the reset time, the more extra virtual users you will need to achieve your goal.

Transaction	Reset	Transaction	Reset

In the example above, the average transaction time and the reset time are both about the same. Each virtual user will only spend half of its time keeping your computing world busy.

If your boss wants the goal stated in terms of number of concurrent virtual users, then just start that number of virtual users plus a few to handle the resetting and reporting downtime, as mentioned above.

When defining the goal you might not have a way to directly measure the number of concurrent virtual users. In that case you can estimate the number concurrent virtual users in your computing world if you know the average number of sessions (i.e., the time a user is considered concurrent) and the average session duration, using Little's Law from chapter three.

ConcurrentUsers = NumOfSessions * AvgSessionDuration

First find the total number of sessions in a peak hour. Then convert the average session duration to units of an hour.

0.05 hours = 180 seconds / 3600 seconds per hour

Then multiply these two values together to find the number of concurrent virtual users.

Here is the same calculation applied to the physical world. Suppose you are building a fast food restaurant and you want to serve 200 people per hour at peak. You also know from previous experience that the average diner spends 15 minutes sitting at a table in this type of restaurant (0.25 hour session duration). How many chairs will you need for all those people?

   200 * .25 = 50 chairs

Those chairs represent the concurrent users, or in this case, concurrent diners.

If your boss wants the goal stated in transactions per second then your job is easy, as during the low-power test validation testing, you'll get a good idea of how many virtual users you need to generate a throughput of X Transactions/second.

Response Time

Measuring throughput without looking at response time is foolish. If you allow infinite response times, then any computer can handle any load. When monitoring response times in a typical load test, you will see this normal progression as the load increases:

1. At a low load the response time looks fine.
2. As you increase the load, at some point the response time will start to climb as a key resource bottlenecks.
3. If you push hard enough the response time will either keep climbing, or start dropping as transactions fail.

The odd thing about response time is that sometimes it is faster to fail, than to succeed. It can be much faster to return an error like: "Zoiks! Database lookup failure" than perform a long, complex query. Once an application is warmed up (processes started, key files in cache, etc.) I've never seen a case where adding more load improved response time.

"If the response time is improving under increased load, then something is broken."
    – Bob's Eighth Rule of Performance Work

For load test goals you need to define an upper limit for acceptable response time. Once you hit that number, then it is pointless to push your computing world harder. You may want to give some thought to how you specify that number. Response time matters a lot to users and how you specify the number will determine the acceptable number of suffering users at peak. You can specify response time as:

1. No response time will exceed X seconds.
2. The average response time will not exceed X seconds.
3. 95% of transactions will take less than X seconds.

The first option ("No response time will...") is very strict and will cost you lots of money to buy all the additional hardware needed to keep the response time for every transaction under this limit. Also, if part of your transaction path crosses the Internet, then that part of the path is totally out of your control. A former colleague often says: "Bad things happen on the Internet".

The second option ("The average...") is much easier to hit, but it has a problem in that many users will still be suffering. Depending on the distribution of response times, this could be half of your users. That's a lot of unhappy users to plan for.

The third option ("95% of transactions ...") is your best bet. This lets you run your computing world harder than the first option and allows less unhappy users than the second option. If you prefer, you can pick a different number than 95%. Some people like 98%, some people like 90%. Just as long as the boss accepts this number, all is well.

Quality of Results

Your load test tool has to have a way of evaluating the quality of responses it gets back from your computing world. Simulating high volume user load can be a tricky business fraught with error. Applications will break under load, security checks will start getting in the way, third parties will have problems, and bad things will start happening on the Internet. The ultimate goal of any load test is to have your computing world smoothly handle a simulated peak load. The term "handle" does not mean to return useless nonsense in a fast an efficient manner. Your load test tool needs to check the retuned results by looking for problems, error messages, and/or missing data.

Internal Meters

Be sure to collect all the internal metering data you can. During a load test, the load can be held very steady. You can choose the exact mix of transactions, so performance meters can be calibrated (At 1000 TX/sec the bamboozle/sec meter = 4000), and explored (transaction X has twice the effect on this meter a transaction Y), with greater ease and precision than when metering a live user load. Your capacity planning efforts can be validated, and you can collect important data to build a model.

Running A Load Test

Now, finally, you have what you need to do the load test. Here is how I'd suggest you proceed.

Begin With Validation Tests

First validate that that the workload you are bringing to the system mimics the live users well enough that you'll have confidence in the results when you emulate the big upcoming peak.

If you are testing the live system, run the test at a time when the load is very low. Adjust the load test so that you are bringing enough work into the system to emulate a moderate load on a not-too-busy day.

Below is an example where a load test was run at moderate load of 500TX/min, late at night when few real users were on the system. The load is turned on and off three times so that we can clearly see the background load that the sleep-deprived late-night users were adding. The chart below shows the overall CPU busy for a key machine.

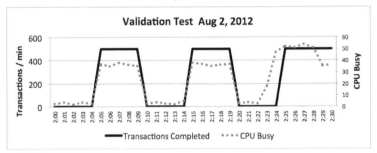

In the first two tests, the transaction load and the CPU utilization moved together nicely. In the third test, the CPU busy started moving upwards before the transactions were sent, so something else was asking this system to do work. We can ignore that third test and then judge if, at 500TX/min, this was a normal amount of CPU consumption compared to the live load. The meters captured during the validation test and the live load do not have to match perfectly. There will always be some noise in the data.

Looking at CPU consumption is a good place to start your validation work, but check your other performance meters as well. See how all the meters match up during the validation test. If some of the meters don't seem to make sense, there are several things to check, improve, and adjust:

- Make sure all the transactions you are sending in are getting valid responses, not error messages.

- Perhaps there is not enough variability in a given transaction. Searching for the word "cow" a million times in a row is not the same as doing a million searches from a randomly chosen list of a thousand different words.

- If you can't seem to drive the transaction rate high enough, perhaps you are having a locking issue. For example, simultaneously updating the same user record from many virtual users can prevent the test from scaling up as everyone is waiting for everyone else.

- Perhaps you need to script additional transactions and add them to the workload mix.

- Perhaps you need to adjust the ratio of the different transaction types in the workload mix.

Keep testing and refining your load until it looks right, runs without error, and returns result that are close enough to what you see on the live system.

Load Tests

With your test validated, now you are ready to try a full-power load test. This is a big event as you are going to push your computing world hard. Things might break, performance automated alerts will go out, dashboards will turn unhappy colors, and, if this is a test on the live system, user performance will suffer. Be sure that everyone is informed well before the test and has an easy way to communicate during the test.

Start the load test at the level you've previously validated. Run at that level long enough so that you have time to check in with the key players to see if their meters are running and everything is as expected. If all is good, then ramp up your load over time until you get to your goal and run at the goal transaction rate long enough to get multiple samples of the internal meters.

Below is a load test that was initially validated at 100 virtual users, with a goal load of 625 virtual users.

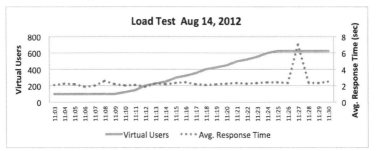

This is a happy load test as the average response time stayed nice and level except for one data point at 11:27. Since everything else looks good, you might choose to ignore that and declare a success. However, when you present your results, it is very probable that someone in the meeting will be fascinated with this odd result. You could rerun the test and hope the event was a one-time thing, or you could do the right thing and figure out what caused that spike in response time.

Below is an unhappy load test, as the more work you brought to the system, the worse the response time got. At 100 virtual users, the average response time was 0.7 seconds. Once we got to 150 virtual users the response time started climbing. That is never good.

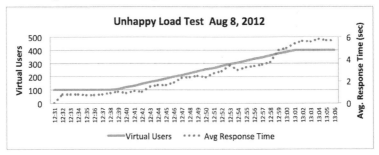

When setting goals for the load test, you should have well defined upper limits for response time and number of errors. Typically the response time goals are a very small multiple of normal low-load response times. So if normal here is 0.75 seconds, then you might have a peak-load goal of no worse that 2X that number, or 1.5 seconds.

Oddly enough, response time can go down under increasing load. This is never a good thing because this only happens when something is failing. It is often faster to fail, than it is to do all the work the transaction requires.

Below is a graph of a bad test where the response time climbs and crashes over and over. This pattern is an artifact of this particular load generation tool. Once this tool hits a certain error threshold, it will reduce the load until the errors subside and then it will ramp up the load again. Regardless of the particular pattern, if you see response time dramatically improving as the load climbs, something is wrong. Start looking for what is failing.

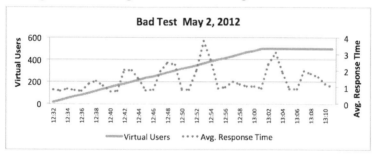

Below is a different chart from the same bad test that shows transactions completed and average response time for those transactions. Notice the lines crossing again and again. The low points are where transactions are failing quickly.

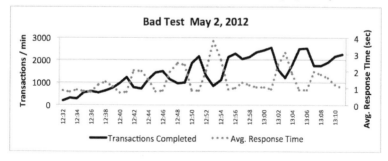

Every load test you ever build or buy will have unique ways of presenting the results and detecting and dealing with errors. Before your first real load test, you should explore the tool, see how it behaves, and understand exactly what the meter is telling you. For example, if the tool gives you a number labeled "transactions", are they started, or completed, transactions? If the tool gives you a number for virtual users, is that the target number or the actual number? Is that number the average during the sample period or the total number at the beginning of the minute? These fine distinctions make a big difference in how much you can deduce from any meter.

After The Load Test
Once the load test finds a point where the response time gets bad and lots of errors are happening, stop and study the results. Let's say your computing world ran out of gas at about 1000TX/minute, and your goal was to get to 1600TX/minute. It can be helpful to run an additional test where you approach the failure point in stages, pausing at each stage long enough to give the internal meters time to get several good samples. So your test might run with an unchanging load for five minutes at 800, then jump to 900, then jump to 1000 TX/min.

Your internal meters at 800 TX/min are approximately half as busy as they will be at your target transaction rate of 1600TX/min. This is a good opportunity to do some quick capacity planning and see what you are likely to run out of. Doing this means you get more information out of each load test, and that means lower costs and less 3am load test runs to wake up for. Running the test at 900 and 1000TX/min allows you to double check your work. I've seen instances where a resource that looked like it was going to be the bottleneck did not increase in proportion to the additional load.

Failures to Avoid and Opportunities to Seize

In no particular order, here are a few final things that have worked well for me and some lessons I've learned. Examine each one. Think about them in the context of your organization, your personality, your duties, and the daily challenges you face. Use what works and discard the rest.

Load Testing Is a Team Sport

Load testing requires the help and cooperation of many people. This is usually extra work done at very inconvenient times. Those people can be ordered to cooperate, but they give you so much more if they understand what's going on and get treated with a little respect. Here are a few good things to do:

- Ask for their help.

- Give plenty of advance notice.

- Explain what you are doing with the test and inquire about any unforeseen difficulties the test might create, or opportunities the test might offer if a small change is made.

- Bring food.

- Share your results after the test.

- Say "Thank You" and mean it.

- Pay it forward by always being helpful to others.

Reality vs. The Lab

It's vastly easier to test the application in its native environment than it is to recreate and test a copy of it in a lab on rented equipment. If you have to go into the lab, expect many delays as you discover just how fussy a computer program can be about the computer it runs on, its surroundings, the placement of files, and network connectivity.

Lab-based Load Test Failures I've Seen More Than Once

The team showed up with *almost* everything they needed. Pack carefully for the trip.

The team showed up with unfinished or poorly tested software. Don't plan to fix it in the lab.

The team assumed that key equipment would be there. They assumed the right version of software and hardware would not only be available, but already be installed for them. They assumed an expert would be available at a moment's notice. Don't assume, check.

The team finally ran the load test successfully after several hardware and configuration changes. Sadly, no one recorded key details of the configuration that finally worked, so the results were meaningless. Take careful notes and make load tests as self-documenting as possible.

The team did not plan how they would reset the system quickly between tests, so they spent 75% of their lab time resetting for the next run. Plan for multiple runs and do what you can to speed up test resets.

Use Checklists

The smallest forgotten detail can ruin a perfectly good load test. Have a checklist and use it. Checklists work for NASA, for surgeons, for pilots, and for load testers.

Ironically, all checklists are incomplete. When you find something missing from the list, take the time to update the master copy of the list.

Communicate During The Test

A full-power peak load test has the potential to be a disruptive event. Before the test starts, open a voice bridge so that all interested parties can follow what's going on and report troubles quickly. Check in with everyone periodically at key points. For example:

- Before testing starts: "Are you ready?"

- When test is first running at low power: "Do you see that load in your meters?"

- As the load is ramping up: "Any problems?"

Time is of The Essence.

Everything you can do to save yourself time, and everything you can do to speed up and automate your testing, is a good thing to do. This allows you to do more testing in a given amount time and to rapidly diagnose problems. During the test many people will be impatiently waiting for you.

Spend time before the test preparing your tools to:

- Start the metering and then the test

- Check if the test and the metering are running as expected

- Rapidly capture every possible clue when the test fails

- Reset things to a known state after a run

- Do rapid performance analysis of the metering data looking for problems and bottlenecks

Clean Up After Yourself

This will not be your only load test. Make sure you have time in the schedule for cleanup. If you are in your own internal lab, or some vendor's lab, leave it nicely picked up when you are done testing. The people who will have to clean up your mess are also the people who will help you set up for the next test. Someday, you'll be back in that lab and need their help again.

Sharpen the sword

After you do a big load test, you should take time to review your notes, logs, and memories looking for things that worked well and things that did not. Improve your tools for next time. This is also a good time to spend time publicly thanking those who helped you.

Chapter 7

MODELING

"The future ain't what it used to be."
- Yogi Berra

This chapter dispels the myth of modeling complexity and shows how modeling performance can save you a lot of time and money.

About Modeling...

There are as many kinds of models as there are PhD candidates to dream them up. For most people, they feature complex math and nearly impenetrable terminology. I'll bet many of them are wonderfully useful. I encourage you, if you so desire, to explore them in other books. In this book we'll look at just two kinds of models: Capacity and Simulation.

Capacity Models

Capacity models are just regular old capacity planning with a bit of a twist. Instead of "find a utilization and scale it," now there is more work to do. In a capacity model you are redirecting the flow of work, adding new work, adjusting the mix of current transactions, or incorporating new hardware. There are more things to count and account for.

To do a capacity model you have to understand what you've got, and then figure out how to adjust the numbers to compensate for the changes you are modeling. It requires performance monitoring, capacity planning skills, simple math and an eye for detail.

Capacity models can do a lot, but they can't predict the response time under load. If you need to know that, then you need a simulation model.

Simulation Models

Simulation models are a funny combination of an accounting program, a random number generator, and a time machine.

They simulate work arriving randomly at a pace you select and then simulate the flow of work though a simulated computing world by accounting for costs and delays at every step. They can run faster, or slower, than real time. They can skip ahead through time when they've got nothing to simulate at the moment. They give you throughput, utilization and response time information for any computing world that you can dream up. The only problem is that they sound scary.

I used to believe that simulation modeling could only be done by super-smart NASA engineers and was only reasonable to do in situations where things had to work the first time or people would be killed and millions of dollars worth of hardware would be destroyed. I used to believe that simulation modeling was incredibly expensive, hard, and time consuming. I was wrong.

I've found modeling to be a useful, and important tool in my toolbox. I taught modeling concepts and a PC-based simulation modeling tool to rooms full of regular people who worked for regular companies, doing the normal work of maintaining and improving commercial systems. From that I learned modeling is doable. The stories I heard from my students about the models their companies relied on taught me that modeling is useful.

Some Modeling Truths
Before I get into model building, here are some surprising truths about modeling.

Modeling Is Necessary
There are two kinds of important performance problems you can't solve without modeling. You can't do performance monitoring, capacity planning, or load testing on un-built systems, as there is nothing to test. You can't use simple capacity planning or load testing to predict future

performance on systems that are about to undergo radical transformations.

In both cases there is a bit of a chicken-or-egg problem as the company wants to know the cost of the hardware for the unbuilt or radically transformed computing world before it is built, but until you build/transform it, you don't have all the data you need to make those projections. This is solvable.

All Models Are Wrong...
George Box once artfully said: "All Models are wrong, some models are useful." So, please take a moment and get over the fact that your model won't generate a perfect result.

Nobody models to a high degree of accuracy because to get that you have to build wildly complex models that model every little thing. You have to put so much time into the model that the business is out of business before the model sees its first run. The 80:20 rule of chapter three applies here. A simple model can give you a ballpark answer. That is often more than good enough to green light a project or size a hardware request.

...Some Models Are Useful
Imagine an inaccurate model where you are guessing at many of the input parameters and unsure about the transaction mix or peak demand. You run the model and, even with the most optimistic assumptions, it forecasts that you'll have to buy somewhere between two and five new servers. If the budget is closed for the rest of the year, then this useful model just saved you a lot of time on that sure-to-fail idea. The thing that makes a model useful is your

confidence that it is accurate enough to answer your
question.

> **"If you have to model, build the least accurate model
> that will do the job."**
> – Bob's Ninth Rule of Performance Work

Modeling Can Be Done At Any Time

All models can be built at different stages of a project's
lifecycle: design, testing, and production. At each stage
there is data available to build a model.

In the design stage, models are built on educated guesses,
the results of quick tests, business plans, and other less than
concrete data. They answer big scale questions like "How
many servers will we need?" and are not all that precise.

In the testing stage, models can be built with better data as
the design is fairly fixed and there is some running software
to meter. Here you can ask small scale questions such as
"Can both these processes run on the same server?" as well
as big scale questions like "Will this configuration handle
the peak?"

In the production stage the entire application and
computing world can be metered and tested against. Here,
with enough work, you can build a model to answer almost
any question.

Models Can Be Built To Different "Resolutions"

At some point in every model you treat some part of your
computing world like a black box. Data goes in, data comes
out, and you don't care about the exact inner workings.
Depending on the question you want answered, the model
can treat any part of your transaction path as that
mysterious black box. It could be as small as a single
communications link or as large as the entire datacenter.

The higher the resolution of the model, the more costly and

time consuming it is to build. Do not confuse high resolution with high accuracy, as they are not the same. A low-resolution model can give you a spot-on accurate answer. For example, if you are modeling your datacenter's Internet connection, you don't care what happens inside the datacenter, you care about how the bandwidth requirements will change as the transaction mix changes.

Modeling Projects Begin With a Question

In the beginning there is an idea, a goal, a mandate, or a proposal that leads to a question. If you can answer that question though simple performance measurement or capacity planning, then do it and be done.

If this is a new application (and thus no metering is possible), or your computing world is changing radically, then you may need to build a model.

The first step to doing that is to really understand the question. Start with what they give you, and then ask very picky questions:

Boss: Will this plan to consolidate systems work?

You: At our seasonal peak load?

Boss: At the seasonal peak.

You: How much should I add to last year's peak?

Boss: Plan on adding 10%.

You: How sure are you of that number?

Boss: Pretty sure, plus or minus 10%.

You: So I should plan for 11% (10% + (10% * 10%)?

Boss: No. To be safe, plan for last year's peak plus 20%.

You: Is there any money available new hardware?

Boss: Not a penny.

Ask all the key players for clarification and additional

information in both positive and a negative ways: "What do you want? What must we avoid?" Keep at it until you really understand the critical success factors such as:

- What success looks like in terms of throughput and response time

- Constraints on budget and time that will limit your options for achieving the goals

- Legal and availability concerns that will limit the configuration of your computing world

- What is politically and bureaucratically possible

To be clear, this is not a license to waste people's time by acting like a three year old asking "Why?" over and over and over. Keep your goal in mind, which is a clearly defined question to answer.

Brainstorm, Refine and Choose

To build a model to find an answer to a question you first have to guess the answer; then you can build a model to see if it is really the answer. To guess the answer, you first brainstorm a list of possible answers and then thin that list down to the best candidates.

Create a List Of Possible Solutions

Start with that question, and your knowledge of your computing world, and come up with a couple of workable solutions. This is the intuitive, creative part of modeling, and it is very much like writing a hit song. There is no step-by-step procedure that will always end up with a great song. However, there are guidelines that will improve your odds of creating a workable solution to your question:

- At first, don't be judgmental. Any idea that, in any way, answers any part of the question is a good one at this point.

- As you are brainstorming, be sure to write things down. The saddest thing is to watch someone struggle to remember, like you do with a fading dream, the key insight that made an idea work.

- Now sift the ideas you have based on key limits and demands of your question. For example, if there is no money for new hardware, then set those ideas requiring new hardware aside, but do not discard them. You may need these ideas later.

- If you have an abundance of ideas that may answer the question, then sort them based on simplicity, risk, and total cost, and take the top three.

- If you have no ideas left that may answer the question, then you should ask the people in charge for guidance as to what in the question can be loosened, ignored, or worked around.

- If you are stuck, go back to those failed ideas you set aside earlier. See if any of them will work for you now.

Refine The Solutions

You should now have a few possible solutions that might work. Before you go through the work to build models, refine your list of solutions by using a bit of simple capacity planning.

To answer the whole question you might need a model, but to figure out that a proposed solution doesn't work can sometimes be seen with simple capacity planning of some small part of the whole question. That sad news might get you to abandon the idea altogether, or it might lead to a modification of the original idea to make it better. Use simple, rapid tools to find problems in your plan before wasting more time modeling a solution that can never work. Let's look at an example.

We are planning to add the workload generated by the new XYZ transaction to a key system. There is no test data yet, but reasonable people agree that, due to its complexity, the XYZ transaction should take 2.5 times the CPU resources of the current BBQ transaction on that key system.

The BBQ transaction consumes 20ms of CPU per transaction, so the XYZ transaction will most likely use (2.5 * 20ms)= 50ms of CPU. At peak load you are planning for 100 BBQ TX/sec and estimating that there will be 20 XYZ TX/sec. On this key system, just these two transactions will use three seconds per second of CPU as you can see below.

TX	CPU	Rate	Total Cost
BBQ	20ms	100/sec	2000ms/sec
XYZ	50ms	20/sec	1000ms/sec

If that machine is a two CPU machine, then this idea is dead in the water.

Seek Out Missing Information

There will come a point where you know most of what you need to know but are missing a key bit of information on throughput, service time, utilization, etc. Remember the various laws introduced Chapter 3 to tease out critical bits of information? These equations can always be rearranged mathematically (e.g. if A=B*C then B=A/C and C = A/B) to find the thing you are missing.

Little's Law

> Mean#InSystem = MeanResponseTime * MeanThroughput

Utilization Law

> MeanUtilization = ServiceTime * MeanThroughput

Service Demand Law

> ServiceTime = MeanUtilization / MeanThroughput

Double Check Your Work

As you are exploring these solutions, be sure to keep looking for a number that rubs you the wrong way or an assertion you can't stop thinking is wrong. Keep asking yourself questions like these.

- Will this work at peak load?

- Can that number really be that low?

- Am I using the right metering data?

- Did I mess up the units in this calculation?

A Note To Beginners

If this is your first time doing this, you are starting from scratch. Don't make the mistake of doing that again next year. Save your report, your notes, and any tools you created to help you write this report. Next time, you'll have a good base to start with and build on. This will save you time and make sure you don't forget things. As the time between peaks goes by, you'll usually find new things to add to the model. Write them down, build them into your performance tools, and file them with all your other modeling data so you don't forget them when you plan the next peak.

"You'll do this again. Always take time to make things easier for your future self."
– Bob's Tenth Rule of Performance Work

Choose Your Model

Now you've got your question, and you've got one or more reasonable looking solutions. Now you need to choose what kind of model you'll use to see if any of the solutions answer the question. There are two fundamental kinds of models: capacity models and simulation models. They both can answer many questions, but only simulation models can give you a predicted average response time as work randomly arrives.

The basic idea of a capacity model is to start where you are and then adjust the numbers based on the planned changes to the work and the computing world. Since there a nearly infinite number of variations, let's take a couple of different examples and work though them.

Capacity Models For New Machines

The Situation

Your computing world is changing. To handle the next projected peak, your sales team has suggested you upgrade your computer to the new model, which they claim is three times faster than your old computer.

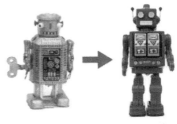

Robot upgrade

Regardless of the sincerity of the sales team and their dedication to truth, the claim that the new machine is three times faster is wrong in the same fundamental way that assuming your SAT scores predict your ability to write a best selling novel. Every time you switch hardware, some parts are faster, some hardly change at all, and occasionally, some parts can run more slowly. It's how your unique application uses those parts that will determine how much more work the new system will handle.

So where to begin?

Start with the simple things. Do all the calculations that you can do simply and easily first. If they work out, then move on to the more detailed and complex work. If they don't work out, then you have to rethink your answer, and you've just saved yourself the time you would have wasted on detailed analysis.

For example, that three times faster number they gave you is usually heavily weighted toward the CPU performance. So capacity plan your current system for your peak load and check to see if it will "fit" into your new system.

Let's say the next projected seasonal peak is 5X busier than a moderately busy day you metered recently. On that day the system was about 30% busy. Do the math (5* 30% = 150%) to see that your old system would be 150% CPU busy at peak. The new machine is 3X as fast as your old machine, and it only has to be 1.5x faster to (barely) handle the load. Chances are you are good to go CPU wise.

If the numbers had been uncomfortably close (e.g., the new machine was 1.7X faster than the old one), then more testing and checking would be in order. Remember, the closer you are to the edge of a performance cliff, the more precisely you have to know your position to stay safe. If it looks like the device in question is going to be over 50% busy, consult the queuing theory section in chapter three to get a rough estimate of the response time penalty you will pay.

Now, dig though each part of the machine to make sure this upgrade will do the job. Do one thing at a time. Take good notes. Write your capacity report as you go.

The Hard Truth About Scaling

For any computer, application, or process you're ever likely to encounter, the following describes the transaction path:

1. Bits go in.
2. Bits are transformed by the CPU.
3. You may have to wait as bits are sent to, or requested from, local storage or some other computer.
4. Bits go out.

It is in step three that your dreams of magical performance increases and simple scaling go to die. Compared to pushing bits around in memory, waiting for data requested from local storage and other computers is tremendously slow. Also, when you upgrade a system, the time to fetch bits from local storage, or another computer, rarely keeps up with the overall speed increase the sales team promised you.

For example, if a process needs to read one record from disk for every transaction, then that IO is may be the biggest throughput limit. Even when you upgrade to a faster CPU, the disk runs at about the same speed, and so the transaction duration does not scale well as you see below.

So, to handle 5X the load with your new machine you may need to add more processes. Any given process can only do so many transactions per second, and that number may not scale up to match the overall speed increase the salesperson claimed for the reasons outlined above. Let's work through an example.

Many of the applications I've worked with had the ability to dynamically add new processes if incoming workload required it. A trick I've used to find the maximum throughput of a process is to start fewer than are normally required and then wait for the user workload to build as the day progresses. I'd watch closely for signs that the transactions are backing up and, when I felt I'd hit the maximum throughput, then I'd start the regular number of processes. Lastly, I do a bit of simple math to calculate the throughput of a process.

- With 2 processes I hit max throughput at 100 TX/sec

- So that gives me: 100 / 2 = 50 TX/sec per process and I know that each transaction takes about 20ms total time as 1000ms / 50 = 20ms

- During testing each process used ~150ms/sec of CPU

- So that gives me: 150ms/50TX= 3ms CPU/transaction

- The CPU on the new machine is three times as fast

- So that gives me: 3ms / 3 = 1ms of CPU estimated per transaction on the new machine

- Each transaction on the new machine will spend 2ms less time computing so the average transaction time will be 20ms - 2ms = 18ms

- So that works out to a max throughput of ~55 transactions per second as 1000ms / 18ms = 55.5555

It can be tempting to display lots of decimal places in the numbers you come up with as that gives the illusion of precision. However, the numbers you started with are typically not all that precise. Furthermore, if the future of your company hangs on a tenth of a transaction per second then you are cutting it way too close for anyone's comfort.

"Ignore everything to the right of the decimal point."
  – Bob's Eleventh Rule of Performance Work

So, on the old machine, each process could handle 50TX/sec, and on the new machine each process can theoretically handle 55TX/sec. Now you see why you'll need more processes to handle the load even though the machine is much faster.

Communications

Just like waiting for bits from local storage, waiting for bits from another computer can take up a big chunk of the overall transaction response time.

CPU	Wait For Bits From Another Computer	CPU

You can do the same basic trick that we just did with local storage to find the max throughput of a given key process.

When doing this work, make sure to lookout for comm errors. You can't eliminate all comm errors, especially if the Internet is involved, but keep an eye on them as you are gathering your data. If there seems to be a significant increase in comm errors while you are gathering your data, that can have a big affect on throughput.

Look at the communications capacity to see if it can handle the projected peak load, which is 5X the traffic that your old system handled on a moderately busy day. Also be sure there is room for this increased traffic on whatever parts of the corporate network these packets flow through.

Local Storage
At the time of this writing, local storage, typically rotating magnetic disks, are the slowest part of any system and the most likely thing to bottleneck.

When upgrading, think of each disk not only as storage space, but as a device that can only give you a finite number of IO's per second. A new 2TB disk that can perform 200 IOs/sec is not the same as four older 500MB disks that can each perform 150 IOs/sec, but together can perform 600 IO/sec.

A single process waiting for disk IO will notice a speed improvement when it is using the faster 2TB disk, but all the processes doing IO will overwhelm the 2TB disk long before they overwhelm the four 500MB disks.

When moving files to the disks of the new system, remember that the size of the file tells you nothing about how many IO's per second the application does to it. If your operating system gives you per-file IO data, then use it to balance the IO load among your disks. If there are no per-file meters, then you need to have a chat with the programmers and take your best guess as to how much IO is going to each file. Once you decide on a plan, move only a small number of files at a time and see how each move goes.

The other thing to consider when balancing disk IO is the IO load of periodically scheduled jobs like backups, overnight processing, end-of-month reports, etc. I've seen systems that were rebalanced nicely for production that became a nightmare when these background jobs were run. These background jobs don't care about response time, but they do have to finish in a certain window of time. Bad things happen when these jobs linger into the daytime and mess up the live user response times. I've never seen a perfect solution to this problem, so favor the live users and balance the best you can.

Memory

Check to see that the memory that comes with the new system is at least as big as the old system. In general, if your old computer had enough memory for a moderately busy day, then it will be fine at peak load. However, I've seen a couple of cases where the memory usage scaled up and down with the load, so look at the memory usage over time on your old system and see how it changes over the day, and from day to day. Memory upgrades are sold in such huge chunks that you don't have to be very precise in estimating memory needs. If you need more, the next step up will be a huge improvement.

Capacity Models For A Changing Workload

The Situation

The makeup of the workload that flows through some part of your computing world is changing. There will be more of this, less of that, and maybe something new. The "part" of your computing world you are modeling can be as small a single process, or as big as the entire computer. In this case let's model a computer with a changing workload. To build the model, we need to understand the workload and the resource consumption caused by that workload.

The Workload

In this section I'm going to offer you many choices because, in your work with models, you will be faced with all these choices. With every choice I offer, look at your current question, what information you have available, what information you can reasonably dig out with some extra effort, and ask yourself: "What gets me closer to the answer I need?" The choices I'm offering you here are a buffet. Choose what works for you to get the job done.

Let's say we want to model a computer that currently handles two different transactions called X and Y. That system will soon also handle a new transaction called Z. You are planning for a future peak where the X, Y, and Z transactions each arrive at a rate of 20/sec. It would seem that you need to model all three types of transactions (X, Y, and Z), but maybe not...

If the ratio of X and Y transactions is staying about the same, you don't really have to think about them as separate, and you don't have to figure out the resource consumption of each transaction. You can simplify the model to just show how busy the machine will be when you add the Z transaction load.

If the ratio of X to Y transactions is changing (more of this, less of that) then you have to understand the resource consumption of each type of transaction, and have clear idea as to how many X and Y transaction will arrive each second. To that, you can then add the Z transaction load.

However, in some cases different very different transactions are really the same. Think about this situation. The X and the Y transactions may be as different to your company as night and day but, on the computer you are modeling, they behave almost identically. Bits come in, bits go out, both transactions burn about the same amount of CPU, IO and comm bandwidth. If you find that different transactions are computationally similar, then you can ignore the differences and simplify the model by thinking of them as all the same.

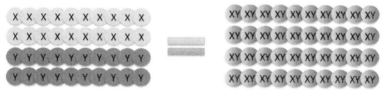

Instead of thinking about a peak per second load of 20 X transactions and 20 Y transactions, you could just view them as 40 XY transactions.

A reasonable person might point out that two transactions never use identical amounts of resources. Think back to the beginning of the chapter... All models are wrong. Build the least accurate model that will answer the question.

No model is perfect. Simplify the model as much as you can. As long as the model gives you an answer that you can trust and explain clearly to others, then you are good to go. To use an analogy, if you are modeling traffic on a busy road you don't have to model (or understand) that the drivers are all very different people going to very different locations because, on that road, they are all just people stuck in their cars.

Lastly, there may be things happening on this system that consume resources but are unrelated to the question. Usually the question allows you to just look at the worse-case scenario and lump all other work into one big resource-consuming blob that can be called such clever things as: *background load*, *base load*, or the ever popular *other*. We'll worry about other in the resource consumption part of this problem.

Getting back to the problem at hand, let's see where we are now. On an average non-peak day around noon, the system we are modeling usually has a steady load of 5 X transactions/sec and 10 Y transactions/sec. The X and Y transactions are significantly different in their resource consumption, and the ratio of X to Y transactions is going to change at our projected peak, so we have to account for them separately in the model.

This is our current and projected workload that we plan to model for this system.

Transaction	Measured at Noon	Projected Peak
X	5/sec	20/sec
Y	10/sec	20/sec
Z	0/sec	20/sec

Resource Consumption

For every unique transaction in your modeled workload you now need to know what resources that transaction consumes. Look back to chapters three and four to find specific hints and techniques to get the data you need. Before you go charging off to collect data, there are a couple of things to consider.

Only collect the data you need to answer the question. At every step of building a model you want to look for ways to simplify and avoid doing unnecessary work. If the question at hand is which CPU upgrade to buy, then focus on the CPU. If it is how many disks are needed, then focus on disks. If it is whether you should select Company A's or Company B's machine, then collect everything.

Now, having just said "only collect the data you need," I'd also like you to look at all the data you get for any looming disasters. The question you are trying to answer is your guide to what you need to collect, but the ultimate goal of any performance work is a smoothly running application at peak load. If your question is focused on CPU, then gather CPU data, but also look at the other data. Take a few minutes to quickly and roughly scale any data to the peak load to see if there is some other disaster looming. Many times I've been asked to focus on one thing, but found the system was just about to run out of something that no one else had thought of or noticed.

Every person doing performance work does so under a

unique set of constraints with a unique set of tools. It may be impossible for you to collect some of the data you need to build the model. If you can't get the data, then you have to guess. Remember, the model itself is a detailed, well thought out guess, so guessing on a particular number you need is not that unheard of. The keys to success when you can't directly meter a key model input are:

Clearly state that this value is a guess in your report.

Use the performance data you can collect to set bounds on the upper and lower range of the number.

Use the Delphi technique (see chapter 3) to get the best estimate you can from the people who are helping you guess.

Sometimes even guessing does not work. This can happen when people can't agree on the number to use, or the boss just isn't comfortable with guessing. In that case you have two paths you can follow. First you can take the biggest value guessed and run the model with it. If the model predicts success, then there is hope that all will be well. If that won't do, then you have to change the question so that the missing number is not needed anymore. If you can't get the data, the model is worthless.

Rate * ??? =

Most of the time the data was not collected at the goal workload rate, so you have to scale it.

Let's say you collected metering data for a given transaction at a rate of eight transactions per second and found it did five total disk reads and burned a total of 200ms of CPU per second. The goal you are shooting for is for 37 transactions per second. The first step is to calculate the scaling factor.

GoalRate / MeasuredRate = ScalingFactor

37 / 8 = 4.6 = ScalingFactor

Then use that scaling factor to scale the measured usage up to the scaled usage.

MeasuredUsage * ScalingFactor = ScaledUsage

5 disk reads per second * 4.6 = 23 disk reads per second

200ms CPU per second * 4.6 = 920ms CPU per second

Once you know your rate and the resource consumption for what you want to model, then plug the numbers into a spreadsheet, and see how well things work.

For this example you'd calculate the total resource costs of the X and the Y transactions at the goal rate of 20/sec. Add to that the estimated (or measured) resource cost of the new transaction Z at 20/sec. Then add the projected "background" or "other" resource costs at peak. Look at the resulting numbers just as you would if they came out of a simple capacity planning exercise. Whether the news is good or bad, write up your findings and present them.

Simulation Models

For a single part of the transaction path you can estimate how busy the hardware is by assuming the workload arrives randomly. With the queuing theory insights found in

Chapter 3, you can come up with a useful estimate of the average response time and throughput.

The trouble is that your computing world is built of many interconnected and interdependent parts. They compete for shared resources and that competition injects massive complexity into modeling the entire transaction path. It is also the case that some parts of the transaction path have more capacity than others, and that causes bottlenecks to form. Those bottlenecks will starve downstream resources for work. All of this together means that it is very hard to predict the average response time of the entire transaction path. For that, you need a simulation model.

Building a Simulation model
Simulation models take some work to set up and require modeling software to run them. They all require four basic kinds of information which can be gathered with the techniques described in this book.

Workload   This is the work the model will be asked to do, e.g., 500TPS of transaction X, and 200TPS of transaction Y.

Infrastructure   These are the things the model will simulate, e.g.: Four servers connected by a gigabit network connection.

Trans. Path   This is how work flows through the systems, e.g.: each of the two front end servers gets half the transactions, they then all go to the validation server, and then on to the payment servers.

Resource   This is the cost of doing the work, e.g.: Each front-end server uses 10MS of CPU, does one disk read, and sends out 2200 bytes to the validation server for every X transaction.

Simulation modeling is scalable. You can simulate a single process, a collection of computers, or the entire datacenter. However, to answer the question, you never have to simulate every little detail. Simulating a small subset of the details often does the trick nicely.

How Simulation Models Work

As I said previously, simulation models are a funny combination of an accounting program, a random number generator, and a time machine. The user interface and features of your software will be different, but all simulation models do fundamentally do the same thing.

Based on your workload data, the simulator generates simulated transactions arriving randomly at a pace you select. It then moves the work through the model. At each modeled point, each transaction arrives to find the needed resource(s) either free or busy. If free, the resource cost is tallied. If busy, the work waits in the queue for service. Once the work completes, the total response time and resource cost is calculated and recorded. The simulated transaction then moves to the next point in the transaction path, and repeats this process until the transaction completes. The simulator keeps simulating new transactions for as long as you told the model to run.

The model does not simulate the deep inner workings of the program. It does not know or care what your code does or what data is passed. It just notes that a transaction arrived, burned some resources, maybe had to wait for a busy resource, and departed. Depending on the complexity of the simulation and the speed of the simulator, models can simulate an entire peak hour of transactions in a few seconds of real time.

Working With The Output Of Simulation Models

At the end of a model run you see charts, graphs, and tables showing throughput, response time, and resource constraints. These take into account the interactions between resources and all the queuing delays. What you get is a detailed guess as to how much work the thing you are modeling can do and what the end users might expect for response time changes as the load goes up.

Just like real applications, models need a warm-up period. The first few simulated transactions will find the simulated disks nearly idle, queues empty, locks unlocked, etc. As the work flows in, queues will build, buffers will fill, and the model will settle down after a short period.

There have been many math geniuses that have spent years trying to find a mathematical way to know when the warm-up period is over and you can start believing the data. To date there is no good mathematical answer.

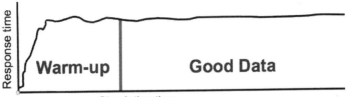

However, just as you do with real metering data during a load test, you can judge that point by eye. Fire up the simulator and let it run. Your eye will clearly note if, and when, the response times and utilizations stabilize. Ignore the data during the warm-up period.

Simulators are driven by pseudorandom number generators that start with a seed value. Run the simulator twice with the same seed, and you'll get identical results. It may be the case that certain seeds generate results that make things look a little better, or a little worse. Once you have a small number of solutions that look promising, rerun them with several different seeds just to double check things. How many runs should you do to be confident? See confidence intervals in chapter 4.

Verification and Validation

At this point you should be a bit worried. A simulation model is a complex thing. There are plenty of opportunities for your errors, and any bugs in the modeling software, to render your models output useless.

How do you learn to trust the simulator's output? How do you learn to trust the model? There are two key things you must do: verification and validation.

Verification asks: "**Did we build the model right?**" Here is where you check:

- Does the model run without errors or warnings?

- Does running a small number of transactions burn exactly the expected modeled resources in the expected modeled places? Pump exactly two transactions though your model and hand check every resource count and utilization number you get to see it is exactly double the resource utilization you specified in your resource consumption data.

- Is the mix of transaction types correct for our workload? Run the model at a low transaction rate, so there are no appreciable queuing delays or resource constraints. Then hand check to see if the model is reporting the expected ratio of X, to Y, to Z transactions.

- Does the output feel right, make sense, and leave you feeling comfortable? Run the model and check to see if all the resources that you are modeling are showing simulated utilization. Does the average response time for transactions go up as you push more simulated work through the model?

All of this detailed work allows you to be more confident that you built the model right, it is working as expected, and you understand the results the model is generating.

Validation asks: **"Did we build the right model?"**

- If we are modeling an existing system, do the modeled results match the metered system? There is nothing like having the model match the live system to inspire confidence in the model. Remember, it will never match exactly. All it has to be is close enough to be a good predictor of future performance.

- Does the model's output make sense to key experts? Humans have an amazing ability to notice when things look wrong. The more people who look at your results and say: "That can't be right," the more you should double-check your model, your assumptions, and your input data.

- Can this model answer the business question that started this whole effort? Go back to the question and see if the results generated by model answers it.

Simulation Model Flexibility

With a simulation model it is easy to change the hardware, move key processes, or change the transaction path. In the real world, doing this is expensive and has real risk. So the changes tend to be big and infrequent.

The downside of simulation model flexibility is you can quickly end up with way too many things to test because it is easy to change the model.

Imagine you have this situation to explore:

- Four server models
- Three application configurations
- Four disk configurations
- Three application configurations

If you test all of them, you'll end up doing almost 150 model runs. Nobody has that much time or patience.

Start by modeling only the biggest and the smallest configurations. For example, run the model that spreads the IO load over two disks (min), and then run it again with ten disks (max), and see if the additional disks made a difference. If more disks didn't help, then there is no sense in testing all the configurations in between. This helps you quickly determine which variables in the model have to be studied carefully.

To Boldly go...
Capacity models are flexible and somewhat easier to do than simulation models. However, they assume a steady state environment and cannot typically deal with algorithms that dynamically tune performance as the load changes. Like any tool, they have limits.

Simulation models can do it all and can give projected response times for complex transaction paths. Regular people can build them, in a reasonable amount of time, with the appropriate tools.

Choose the modeling technique based on the question you are trying to answer.

Always, begin, and end, with the question.

Chapter 8

PRESENTING YOUR RESULTS

"I never said most of the things I said." - Yogi Berra

This chapter teaches you how to present your results so that they are understood and are believable.

To Reveal The Future...

When presenting your results, in many ways you are like the Crystal Seer above. Perhaps the turban and the crystal ball would be a little over the top for your presentation in conference room three, but overall this is not a bad metaphor. When doing performance work, you are uncovering a hidden truth few can see, and predicting the future.

We have all seen a poorly explained truth go down in flames and a beautifully told lie carry the day. If the inmates are running the asylum where you work, then they are most likely very good at presenting their very bad ideas. How clearly and convincingly you present your results determines how successful you are. If this were a book on learning to fly, this chapter would be called "Landing."

To be clear, this is not generic advice on pubic speaking. You can find that elsewhere.

This chapter is a collection of hints on presenting performance results that have worked for me throughout the years as I've presented my results to both friendly and skeptical audiences of managers, technical staff, and executives all the way up to the CIO/CEO level.

I'll suggest some design considerations for your presentation, give some hints on useful preparations to do, and finally offer some advice on giving the presentation.

Designing Your Presentation

These are some things to keep in mind when you have the answer to the question in your hand, and now you get to share the news.

Money Changes Everything

Sometimes performance work is all about the customer: "What do we need to handle the seasonal peak with reasonable response time?" Sometimes performance work is all about the money: "Can we cut 30% of our IT budget?" When it is all about the money, you have to have some financial numbers to work with that everyone agrees upon. Specifically, you need a target amount to save and the relevant costs of the major pieces of hardware in your computing world. Get those financial numbers first, and make sure that everyone is in agreement on them. Now go do your performance work.

For a money-centered question, design your talk to lead with the money, because that is what your audience is focused on. Then talk about what is possible and what, if any, pain will result. For example:

- The goal was to cut the IT hardware budget by 30%. That can be done, and 11 months out of the year all will be well. However, at your seasonal peak, my data predicts horrible response times.

- I believe you can save $250K by making the following changes with no change to your average response times.

When looking at the cost of lost business, it can be useful to look at the lifetime value of a customer, not just the cost of "losing" X transactions.

For example: Imagine a grocery store refuses a return on a bad can of peas. It saved a $1.29 by doing so. However, if that customer buys $200 of groceries a week, 50 weeks a year, and lives near that store for five years, then the lifetime value of that customer is about $50,000. What is the real cost of losing a customer due to slow response time issues?

Proof
As Carl Sagan once said, "Extraordinary claims require extraordinary evidence." Look at your results and conclusions and ask yourself how your audience will react.

The more disruptive, shocking, or expensive your conclusions and recommendations are, the more backup data you need and the more effort you want to expend in making an airtight case. If you are claiming bacon is good for you, then you will have an easier time with the National Pork Producers Board than with a group of vegan cardiologists.

However, just because you have 30 backup slides for your shocking revelation, doesn't mean you need to show them all. Pay attention to your audience. Once you've convinced them, forget the remaining 24 backup slides, and move on to your next point.

The Nature of Truth

When preparing to present your report, there can be tremendous pressure to lie. Your work may help justify a purchase everyone wants to make or force unpleasant changes that no one wants to endure. The politics can get *very* serious.

First and foremost, stick tightly to the data you collected. It is the truth. Everything you do, say, and recommend flows from it. Never change that data. Never cherry pick the "good" numbers. Never ignore the bad numbers. If the powers that be order you to change that data, then start looking for another job because this is not the place anyone wants to work.

Be open to other interpretations of the data. If they do not violate the performance laws in chapter 3, they may be valid. A device being 50% busy is a fact. What that fact means depends on the question at hand and the business realities that you have to live within. I've done performance work at companies where 30% busy on a peak day was a crisis and others where 95% busy was the norm. Both companies were doing wildly different things with their machines, but they, and their customers, were quite content with the performance they were getting.

Simplify

You've done weeks of monitoring, calculation, and testing, and now you've got to explain your work to people who have been (for the most part) blissfully ignorant of your efforts and struggles. There is the natural tendency to show

the detail and talk at length about how hard you worked.
Don't do that.

It takes an incredible amount of ingenuity, work, skill, and
craftsmanship to lift a raw diamond out of the Earth and
craft it into a sparkling gem. The same is true of your work
on this performance project. In both cases, the end product is
prized for its clarity. That clarity comes from the internal
structure, the lack of flaws, and the raw material you
discarded. When writing and presenting be a minimalist.

You will be presenting to people who have natural limits.
Most people, as a rule, are not that good at holding several
numbers in their head simultaneously. People also have a
finite ability to give a damn about what you are saying.
When you exceed that limit, they stop listening, even if you
are explaining how to make perfect $20 bills on a laser
printer. What follows are some goals to strive for when
crafting a presentation.

Eliminate anything extraneous, as every new thing takes
energy to understand. For example, your system might have
15 tuning parameters, but when only three of them matter to
this question, put the rest of them (if you include them at all)
in an appendix. This gets them out of the main flow of your
presentation, and yet it shows you did your due diligence.

Make sure that each point you make requires your audience
to remember no more than two numbers at the same time.

Having a nicely designed table of numbers is fine, as no memorization is required.

Use consistent terms and introduce the least number of new terms possible. Call a "dog" a "dog" all the way though your presentation. Every new and unfamiliar term you introduce is one more plate they have to mentally keep spinning as you are building your next point.

Since graphs are a key element of most performance presentations, do your audience a favor and label your graphs consistently. Put a title and a legend on each graph, and put them in the same place. Label the X and Y axis. Strive to use a common unit (bits vs. bytes) in all your graphs. Use consistent colors so they quickly learn, for example, that the metered values are always blue, the projected values are always red, and the theoretical limit line is always black.

Lastly, establish a pattern in your presentation so people know what to expect. For example, imagine you had capacity planned the performance of a key computer at a future peak. In your presentation, for each subsystem of that computer, show where you are now, then show the projected peak, then state if this will be a problem, and lastly describe any proposed changes to work around the problem. People like a repeating pattern of information in a presentation. They find this comforting and an aid to overall understanding.

The Invisible Presentation
If your audience has trouble seeing what you are presenting, then it is harder for them to understand your wisdom.

Use a big font (24-30 point), that is easy to read (no funky fonts), and has high contrast (black letters on a white background). Save the small fonts for your written summary, and avoid colored fonts on a colored background like the plague.

| Hard To Read | Hard To Read | |

In most meetings a significant part of the audience can't see the bottom 25% of your slide due to the people in front of them. Put the good stuff at the top of the slide. Reserve the bottom for things that are less important to the question at hand, like the page number or the snazzy corporate artwork.

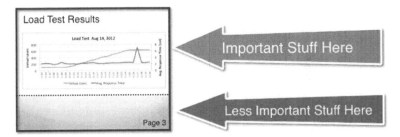

Depending on where you live, seven to nine percent of men and 0.4% of women are red/green colorblind, be sure not to make these the two the most critical colors on your graphs. Also, everyone is colorblind when looking at a black and white printed copy of your presentation.

Preparing For Your Presentation
In addition to having a perfect set of slides and a well written report, there is a mental game to be played as well.

Build Your Faith In Your Results
Your results and conclusions may, or may not, be correct. Mistakes happen. Things are missed. Calculations are botched. Data can be corrupted. You are usually keenly

aware of all of these things just before you have to present your results. Worry creeps into your mind like a cold fog, and you can find yourself unsure you know anything at all.

There is only one way to prevent this. Start by accepting the fact that you are a regular, carbon-based life form fully capable of screwing up, and then do the hard work necessary to build a rock-solid faith in your results and conclusions. If you don't deeply trust in the results, then that lack of trust will show on your face, and whatever you say won't matter. If they don't believe you, your results are worthless. This is especially true high up the org chart as they don't have time to comb through all your data.

Check everything. Check it twice. Look for inconsistencies. If you use a tool to boil down your performance data, recheck a few values to be sure the tool is working. Present your results to a trusted co-worker to debug your analysis. Have someone else look for typos, misspelled words, and grammar glitches. Ninety-nine percent of this work will find nothing amiss, but the work is not wasted. You now have a rock-solid faith in your results, and  your presentation has a few less booboos for your adversaries to use against you.

Practice
It is a natural human reaction to avoid difficult things, and that is why most people never practice their presentations before they give them. This is unfortunate and leads to many overlong, boring, confusing, and generally bad presentations.

You need to practice. Really.

When you practice, say the words out loud, don't just think them. You use a different part of your brain when you speak, and that gives you another chance to notice problems in your logic and in your material. Do you doubt me? Have you ever had some thought that sounded reasonable inside your head but sounded monstrously stupid once you said it out loud? I rest my case. You need to practice. It may feel silly to stand up in an empty room and present to no one, but you need to do this. I've been presenting for over 30 years, and I still do this with new material. It helps me every time.

One key thing to practice is getting any presentation equipment you need set up. I can tell you from painful experience that this is important. I remember the flop-sweat trickling down my forehead as a room full of people watched me struggle with a projector. That very, very bad day taught me to always get to the meeting room early and figure out those little things that can make you look like a big idiot.

No Bad Surprises

Never plan to surprise the person responsible for a problem in a public meeting. The goals of performance work are measured in response time and throughput, not in how much drama you create in the conference room when you point your accusing finger at the unsuspecting culprit.

When you locate a problem, the first person you should find is the person who is responsible for that part of the computing world, and discuss that problem with him or her. Why? That person may know a lot more about that part of your computing world than you do, and may have further insights as to the root cause and the reason(s) why things are done this way. Often, I find that when I privately share my concerns and ask for help in crafting a list of possible solutions, that person is quite willing to be helpful.

I have made the mistake of not involving the person I believed was responsible for the problem and have suffered these consequences, usually in this exact order:

1. The person responsible for that part of the computing world gets angry and defensive and works relentlessly to tear down my work and credibility.

2. That person points out my ignorance and further points out the real problem is caused by some other part of the computing world owned by a different person. Now there are two angry people in the room.

3. Now the manager becomes angry with me for creating tension among the staff.

It always works better when I talk to the responsible person privately well before I write up my recommendations. We look at the problem and explore solutions. Then I can walk into the meeting and say something like: "The problem is here, and after working with Drew, we have a few ideas on how to improve the situation."

The Hidden Agenda

In all talks there are two agendas: **surface** and **hidden**. The surface agenda is the subject of your talk. It is in your slides. You say it out loud. The hidden agenda (e.g., keep my job, get new hardware) is why you are really there. It is never spoken out loud. It is not on the slides, but it is important to you.

When you are presenting, if things start going badly and it is not clear what to do next, remember your hidden agenda. This can keep you from committing career suicide over a point you later realize was small potatoes.

The Inconvenient Truth

There will be times when the meters and your expert analysis show that bad things are in the future. The company is looking at big changes, spending massive amounts of money, and enduring very disruptive fixes. I have seen decision makers on multiple occasions, when presented with unrelenting bad news, simply reduce the scaling factor or lower the desired goals so that the problem simply evaporates. The essential nature of business is risk-and-reward. Sometimes a business will just have to hope that next year will be better, but sometimes what you are watching is a very human reaction to staggeringly bad news.

When people are presented with bad news, that contains no possibility of escape, a significant fraction of them will go into denial regardless of the evidence. The key to greater acceptance of your message is to present the bad news with a possible solution, or at least a way of improving the situation.

"The sky is falling, but your umbrella protects you."

"The XYZ server will run out of CPU at peak, but we can mitigate most of that that by…"

"Always serve bad news with a side order of possible solutions."
– Bob's Twelfth Rule of Performance Work

Giving Your Presentation
Presenting performance results and working through a list of possible solutions has some unique challenges.

Presenting Up The Org Chart
The bigger the problem, and/or the bigger the cost to fix it, the higher up the management chain you will present. If you are used to talking just to your manager, this can be a little daunting. Have courage.

As you move up the org chart, simplify and focus your slides. You are not doing that because they are idiots. You simplify because they are looking at a bigger picture, and they are used to hearing well-vetted presentations. In general, the higher you go, the more graphs and the less numbers you'll use. Bring your backup data as people will often pick something you presented and ask a few deeper questions about it, mostly to see if you really know what you claim to know.

At each level, seek out tips on presenting to the person at the next level up and tune your talk accordingly. Ask simple questions like: "*What works (or fails) when presenting to...?*" or "*What are they like?*" You might find out that person is rude to everyone. Knowing that in advance is very helpful.

Less Is More

Some questions have too many answers. I've watched quite a few meetings spin out of control when the group started open discussion, and participants became confused as they sorted through the myriad of possible choices, while adding new ones on the fly.

There is an interesting book called The Paradox of Choice by Schwartz that points out that the typical human response to too many choices is to make no choice at all.

Offer people three types of food to sample and some of them will choose to buy something. Offer people 30 types of food to sample and far fewer of them will choose to buy anything. More choices often cause people to believe that it is unlikely that they will pick the right, or best, choice.

When presenting ideas on how to fix the problem, I like to offer people two choices that are clearly named and differentiated. If other ideas pop up over the course of the meeting, that is fine, but I keep them clearly labeled and make sure they are never comparing more than three solutions at any one time.

---

*"**Never offer more than two possible solutions or discuss more than three.**"*
    – Bob's Thirteenth Rule of Performance Work

To Tell The Truth

If you are presenting your findings and you don't know something, admit it directly and, if it's important, add it to your to-do list and move on. Don't try to hide your ignorance. The decision makers need to have confidence in you. A big part of that confidence is setting a clear line between what you know and what you don't know.

When pressured by others to hide an inconvenient truth, you can emphasize other things, and you can even leave the inconvenient truth out of your presentation, but **do not lie.**

Leave The Judgments To Others

When you present, you are not a superhero striking down evil. You are not an arbiter of good design. You are not there to make yourself look big by making others feel small.

You are a member of the team, dispassionately presenting well-checked information and potential solutions for problems. Stick to the facts, and leave the judgments to others.

I have seen presentations where the speaker delivered the bad news in a mocking and sometimes directly insulting way that hurt group cohesion and deeply offended people in front of their peers. That approach did not aid in answering the question, but it did unleash a wave of back-stabbing and other bad behavior. Every time I have seen someone be intentionally cruel or hurtful to a co-worker, it has not worked out well for them, especially in the long run.

"Always tell the truth in a kind and helpful way."
            – Bob's Fourteenth Rule of Performance Work

The Five-Minute Trick

More times than I can count, I've been told I have an hour to present my findings and then, at the last minute, have found out that "Mr. Big Cheese is running late" and I'm either being bumped from the schedule altogether or cut back to a small fraction of the time I was originally allotted.

For a critical talk I always prepare a second, totally separate presentation that lasts no more than five minutes, and I offer that to whoever is doing the scheduling for the meeting. 99% of the time that offer gets gratefully accepted. Often, Mr. Big Cheese is intrigued with what I have to say in those five minutes, and I'm asked to go into more detail, while the scheduler goes off to tell someone else that they've been cut from the schedule.

This short presentation is not just going though your slides faster. It is a completely different presentation developed, edited, and optimized to deliver in that brief time. Please don't start whining that you can't possibly do justice to your months of detailed work and analysis in five-minutes. I've successfully given executives presentations this brief:

> *"You will easily make it through your seasonal peak.*
> *The details are in my report."*

> *"The fix for your current problem is moving one*
> *very busy file to three new disks. Your staff*
> *knows what to do."*

As the performance person you can make a big impression when you are prepared to move swiftly, and can help keep the executives running on time. That positive impression lasts a long time and is good for your career.

When The Tension Is High

Sometimes the success or failure of your company hangs on your results. When the stakes are high, and everyone is hoping for good news, while preparing that presentation you might want to think about going to the movies. Specifically an old-school, action movie, like Indiana Jones.

A big reason audiences enjoy an action movie is that they are reasonably sure from the onset that they will like the ending. They are sure that the hero will triumph, and the wrongs will be righted.

There is a temptation to use a dramatic style when presenting the results of your work because you naturally want to tell a story that builds in excitement and drama and finishes with thunderous applause. That is a fine thing to do, but it works much better if you tell them very early in the presentation that all will be well. Then the audience can relax and enjoy the ride. So start your talk with something like this:

> *With the current configuration, we will not be able to*
> *handle the upcoming peak. However, I've identified the*
> *bottlenecks and I have workarounds to propose for all of*
> *them. Let me show you what I've found.*

I have seen presentations, without this early calming statement, go badly. When the presenter was about half way through the list of all the serious problems ahead some participant will start angrily demanding something like: "**Are we screwed?!?**", "**Is there a fix?!?**" This is not what you want.

~~Great~~ Reasonable Expectations

People do not remember everything you tell them, even if you do a great job, use interesting materials, and have an audience with motivation to learn. For any presentation you can reasonably assume the audience will only retain:

- 3-5 concrete facts
- A general understanding of what you presented
- An impression of you as a person

The 3-5 concrete facts are the ones most interesting to them. You can influence that choice by repeating the key facts and telling your audience why these points are important rather than just assuming they will magically know that.

The "general understanding" part of what they remember is like a hard rain in the desert. The water forms streams that erode the land, but the water quickly dries up, or soaks in, leaving only the changed landscape. Those new channels will direct and aid the flow of water when the rains come again. Because of this general understanding, the next time they get this information it will seem familiar, and they will retain more of it in long-term memory.

It is the impression of you that lasts the longest, so try very hard to be helpful, accurate, insightful, creative, and clear. Try very hard not to be a jerk.

Studies show that if you refresh someone's memory of the key points of your talk about 24 hours after learning has completed, the long-term retention rate is greatly improved. Try to find a way to do this when the situation demands that they take action on specific information.

Finally

The single biggest "trick" I use in every talk I've every given is to care about the people in the audience. This is not a trivial closing thought to fill the page.

This is a core truth. You can tell when someone cares about you, and you can tell when they don't. You naturally give more attention and show more compassion to people who care about you.

In the time just before you start, take a moment and let yourself focus on deeply caring about the audience. Care about their needs and concerns. Care about the fact that they have been sitting in meetings for two hours before you started. Care about them as people. Caring connects you to them in a powerful and positive way.

Presenting Your Results

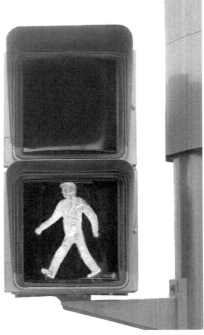

Appendix

BOB'S PERFORMANCE RULES

"It's like deja vu all over again." -Yogi Berra

This appendix reviews and expands on the performance rules sprinkled in this book.

What a Long Strange Trip It's Been...

I've done performance work for many companies and government agencies working with people at every level of the power structure. I started noticing what worked and common patterns of behavior. Below, are the collected rules I presented throughout this book with some further illumination.

The less a company knows about the work their system did in the last five minutes, the more deeply screwed up they are.

I figured this out very early in my career and used it as a very successful metric to help me estimate how much work the job would entail. I would just ask them how busy the system was in the last five minutes.

If the person I asked had a ballpark estimate that they quickly confirmed with some meter, I'd know they were most likely in basically good shape performance-wise. If they had no idea, or only knew the answer to a resolution of an entire day, then I was pretty sure that there would be plenty of performance related ugliness to discover within.

What you fail to plan for, you are condemned to endure.

High availability and consistently great performance happen because people think about, and plan for, the future every day.

Some organizations just stare down at their shoes, never lift their gaze to look into next week, or think about the next peak. The best organizations start planning for the next peak right after the one they just sailed trough.

Most corporations only learn through pain.

We usually get the flu because we touch our nose and eyes and don't wash our hands enough. We know that, and yet we keep doing it over and over again. On the other hand, you only have to touch something hot once, and you never make that mistake again.

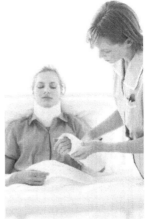

Companies behave just like that. When they get burned, they learn. If the group that has to do the work and spend the money to fix a problem gets burned, it will fix that problem if at all possible. If that problem only inconveniences others, and the fix required is non-trivial, or costs money, 99% of the time they would do exactly nothing.

If they don't trust you, your results are worthless.

As any hardware vendor knows, their advice to buy more equipment is automatically suspect. Internal advice to spend money is also suspect, as who doesn't want the latest, greatest hardware? You have to build trust if you want them to pay attention to your findings. Without trust, they will not believe you and will not push for the changes needed to avoid the troubles ahead. Without trust, you might as well just go home.

Always preserve and protect the raw performance data.

When I have made the mistake of editing the raw performance data it has not worked out well. To be clear, I never edited it to change its meaning or hide the truth. That would be stupid.

When I've deleted raw data to clean up, I ended up suffering later when the question changed. When I edited raw data for easier import, I'd sometimes end up mangling the data itself. Always edit a copy of the raw data. Never delete your raw data.

The meters should make sense to you at all times, not just when it is convenient.

There are meters that are just useless and the good news is that, in my experience, they are consistently useless. You quickly learn to ignore them. All other meters tell their version of the truth in a consistent way.

More times than I can count, I've noticed one meter that disagreed with all the others. When four out of five meters tell you one thing, take the time to understand why the fifth meter disagrees. That will keep you from making big mistakes and lead you to a deeper understanding of what the meters are telling you.

To a corporation, nothing is more important than money.
Follow the money.

When indecisive people are managing your computing world, or you yourself are unsure as to what is the best course, follow the money.

In the absence of direction, notice what directly brings in the money, and you can't go wrong making that the primary focus of your performance work.

If the response time is improving under increased load, then something is broken.

I have never seen a case where a running application sees its response times drop as more load is added, with the rare exception of applications that dynamically add resources (such as server processes) when the load increases.

Algorithms rarely work better under increasing load for a simple reason. Programming projects are notoriously late, and when late, performance optimizations are the first things to be cut. So, look for errors, or dysfunctional behavior, when things magically get faster under heavy load.

If you have to model, build the least accurate model that will do the job.

Why make things harder than they need to be? The more precise your model the more detailed resource and transaction path information you need. Gathering that is the hard part of modeling.

There are some people who should not build models, as they can't accept inaccuracy. If those people are managing you as you build the model, then prepare to suffer.

You'll do this again. Always take time to make things easier for your future self.

In performance work, there is often lots of waiting to do between peaks or while tests are running. I always use some of that waiting time to look for better ways of gathering data, analyzing data, and turning it into presentable information.

Many of the things that can affect performance can be both unlikely and time-consuming to look for, so you tend not to look for them. When I find these things, I figure out a way to check for them and add that to my tool called UnlikelyThings. I let that tool do the hard work for me.

Ignore everything to the right of the decimal point.

There is always uncertainty in the results generated by performance work. Some meters just sample the data, some count everything, and some start early or late. Reporting results like "37.238" is always a waste of time and usually a bit of a lie.

Report the integer part and ignore the fractional part. If you are so close that the fractional part matters, then you are too close for comfort.

If you have to report the fractional part, show a consistent number of decimal places in all your results.

Always serve bad news with a side order of possible solutions.

There is not a manager on Earth who wants to hear, or reacts well to, unrelenting bad news. When driven into the corner, some will come out swinging and fight you tooth and nail on every depressing detail you have to offer.

Assuming there is some good news to deliver, start with some good news, or at least tell them that there is some good news coming. This relaxes the tension somewhat and makes your job easier.

Never offer more than two possible solutions or discuss more than three.

People usually don't approve a solution that they can't understand. They can't understand your solution if they can't remember it. They can't remember it because humans can usually hold at most three ideas in their head at the same time. Too many choices quickly leads to rapid non-decision and confusion.

As I learned in my childhood from Schoolhouse Rock, "Three, it's a magic number."

Always tell the truth, but in a kind and helpful way.

Never use your performance skills as a basis for saying harsh things about the design or implementation of your computing world. Show your results, identify the problem areas, suggest improvements, but stick to the facts and don't denigrate individuals or use harsh descriptors such as, "stupid". People you work with usually built that computing world and they have families.

Harsh words never help, but they can backfire on you. When attacked, people want to protect the job that takes care of their families. They look for ways to stop you, and nobody needs that.

Appendix

IMAGE
CREDITS

"It ain't over till it's over." - Yogi Berra

This chapter contains the acknowledgments and attributions required for the images used in this book.

About The Images In This Book

All the images in this book were either created by the author, are copyright free, are licensed under Creative Commons attribution 2.0 generic license, or are from licensed collections.

The cover photo is a beloved toy robot perched on top of the beloved Apple iMac on which I wrote this book.

The images that require attribution are listed below in the order you find them in each chapter, one line per image. Each line contains a description followed by the attribution.

Book Cover
Robot: Bob Wescott & Anna Macijeski

Acknowledgments
Flowers: Fleur Suijten

Preface
Keys: Musk

Chapter 1
Cuckoo Clock: Tatiana Gerus
Voter Line: Adria Richards
Old Meters: Pieter Schepens
Two guys: RDECOM

Chapter 2
Ice Cream Scoop: Bob Wescott & Anna Macijeski
Bottleneck: Noah Dibley
Paper Airplane: Roel Kuik
Hurricane Model: N.O.A.A.
Damaged Road: Jim Greenhill

Chapter 3
Lightbulb: Davide Guglielmo
Experts Talking: Fred Thompson

Chapter 4
Stopwatch: Jean Scheijen
XKCD Comic: XKCD.com
Hygrometer: Iwan Beijes
Jets: Simon_sees
Model train: Ferdinand Mels
Fire Truck: Kenn Kiser

Chapter 5

Pouring Coffee:	Christopher Meder
Clock Closeup:	Darren Hester
Cliff Edge:	Orin Zebest
Tachometer:	LifeSupercharger
Under The Bed:	Sarah Fleming
Firefighters:	DVIDSHUB
Train Gate:	Ken Kiser

Chapter 6

Subway crowd:	TwoWings
Lightbulb:	Davide Guglielmo
Robot:	SeeMann
Rugby:	Leena Ontask
Glass of wine	Stuart Webster
Chair:	epSos.de
Control Room:	Highways Agency
Trash bin:	Zsuzsanna Kilian

Chapter 7

Model Windmill:	Joe King
Climate display:	NASA Goddard Space Flight Center
George Box:	David MC Eddy
Question Man:	Marco Bellucci
Whiteboard:	Jon Gosier
Magnetic Disk:	Marcin Bartowski
Orange Conveyor:	U.S. Department of Agriculture
Magnifying Glass:	YellowJ

Chapter 8

Crystal Seer:	Ali
Crystal Ball:	Penywise
Peas:	Daniel Fuhr
Worried Guy:	Christophe Fouquin
Three Apples:	davharuk
Clock:	Chris Gilbert
Two Boys:	Sonya Etchison

Chapter 9

Walk Sign:	Davide Guglielmo
MouseTrap:	David Loudon
Distrust:	Scott McLeod
Mountie:	Forest Runner
Tachometer:	Brian Snelson
Money:	Alvimann
Paper Airplane:	Svilen Milev
Waitress:	Alan Light
Yellow Leaves:	John Talbot

Chapter 10

Camera:	Moogoo

Made in the USA
San Bernardino, CA
06 May 2014